IMAGE
Marketing

IMAGE
Marketing

Using Public Perceptions to Attain Business Objectives

JOE MARCONI

Printed on recyclable paper

American Marketing Association
Chicago, Illinois

NTC Business Books
a division of *NTC Publishing Group* • Lincolnwood, Illinois USA

Library of Congress Cataloging-in-Publication Data

Marconi, Joe.
   Image marketing : using public perceptions to attain business
objectives / Joe Marconi.
      p.   cm.
   Includes bibliographical references and index.
   ISBN 0-8442-3504-0 (alk. paper)
   1. Corporate image.   2. Advocacy advertising.   3. Public
relations.   4. Mass media and business.   I. Title.
HD59.2.M37   1996
659.2—dc20   95-46960
                                                                    CIP

Published in conjunction with the American Marketing Association, 250 South Wacker
Drive, Chicago, Illinois, 60606.

Published by NTC Business Books, a division of NTC Publishing Group
4255 West Touhy Avenue
Lincolnwood (Chicago), Illinois 60646-1975, U.S.A.
67890 BC 987654321

For Karin
Thanks for waiting.

CONTENTS

SECTION **I**

Image Marketing

CHAPTER **1**

CHAPTER 2

The Tools: *What* People Think of You vs. *How* People Think of You   **25**

CHAPTER 3

The Market Climate and the Halo Effect   **55**

CHAPTER 4

The Ups and Downs of Endorsements and Sponsorships   **75**

CHAPTER 5

Seriously Not Taking Yourself Too Seriously   93

At a Glance: Seriously Not Taking Yourself
   Too Seriously   102

CHAPTER 6

The Media and the Budget: What Should
Image Marketing Cost?   105

The Medium and the Message: Where to Go and Why   107
Competing for Time and Space   108
Make the Media Fit Your Image   110
The Theater of the Mind   114
At a Glance: The Media and the Budget   126

CHAPTER 7

When the Product Is Bigger than a Breadbox   129

Marketing the Military   131
Marketing Religion   135
Marketing Higher Education   140
Marketing the City, the State or the Country   143
Marketing Doctors, Lawyers and Political Figures   151
At a Glance: When the Product Is Bigger than a Breadbox   166

CHAPTER

SECTION ▐▐

The Image Marketing Casebook

CHAPTER

CHAPTER 10

A Crash Course in Image Marketing

Bibliography and Reference
Credits
About the Author
Index

In an era of rampant tabloid journalism and instant celebrity, the issue of style over substance has never been more dramatic. Substance is nice, but style is what sells—big. Buying decisions, viewing decisions, voting decisions are all showing a marked emphasis on *image*.

Obsession fragrance ads feature nude models in surreal scenes suggesting an *image* of danger and sensual excitement.

Candidate Bill Clinton played his saxophone on a television talk show and conveyed a good-natured, relaxed and confident *image* that was a sharp contrast to his proper, buttoned-up, perhaps pompous opponents.

Michael Jordan and Nancy Kerrigan, as well as other athletes and performers, receive lucrative endorsement deals far less because of their talent or athletic abilities than because of the *image* they represent in the minds of advertisers and the public.

That Snickers was "the official snack food of the U.S. Olympic team" was not a testament to the taste, value or quality of the candy bar, but to the *image* M&M/Mars wanted to present of its company with the support of the team.

Presenting a good public face has always been important and business has always recognized the value of a good reputation. But the 1990s and the period beyond suggest an era where image takes on an additional, critical importance, as Disney, Apple, IBM, Sony, Playboy, Time Warner, American Express, Rupert Murdoch and Donald Trump will find their *image*—how it looks and how it sells—of as much concern to their banks as their marketing plans and their business plans.

Media-smart and public opinion-sensitive entities are paying attention to what is emerging as *image marketing*—*making your name, your reputation and public perceptions help build greater awareness and market share.* This book will offer a guide to what should and shouldn't be done to successfully market an individual, a company, an entity or a product image, by exploring specific examples of what has worked and what hasn't.

Some pundits compare a positive, high-profile to a "lot of flash." And, of course, sometimes that's all it is. Those who try to overtly cultivate a good image are often regarded as almost sinister or at least deserving of suspicion. This book, however, will take the high road, and assume that a good image is the reflection of a good product, a good company, a good person and/or good work. The pundits don't yet seem to have much to say about substantive people and companies that can stand up to scrutiny. Under such circumstances, misrepresentations and even outright lies have been advanced and reputations ruined. Accuracy and ethics don't seem to have the value they once had and competitors, opponents, critics and often the media have adopted something of an "all's fair" attitude in their respective quests to become number one.

This book is for marketing professionals, managers, or individuals who need to create, maintain or change their public image—or that of a company, business or a professional services enterprise. For the most part, trade terms and jargon have been avoided.

Some of the material here will seem pretty basic; other information is likely to have fallen outside the reader's professional experience so far. The rule followed has been not to assume. Some people engaged in marketing for a decade or more have never written a marketing plan (or perhaps even seen one). That's not intended to be a criticism but, rather, an explanation of why the step-by-step approach is sometimes recommended and examples presented.

For contributions, assistance, encouragement and support, special thanks to Francesca Van Gorp at the American Marketing Association, Rich Hagle at NTC Publishing Group, Michael Jeffers, Steve Kerns, Lonny Bernardi, Rich Girod, Guy Kendler, Ginny LaVone, David Bender, Steve Jareo, Keroff & Rosenberg Advertising and to Karin Gottschalk, without whose assistance this book would have gone to press from a stack of pages written in ink on yellow legal pads.

Joe Marconi
Western Springs, Illinois

INTRODUCTION

Victoria's Secret. Calvin Klein. McDonald's. Playboy . . . When a word is worth a thousand pictures, that word has "image marketability."

Few of our most important and most successful names were instant successes. Countless stories tell of planning, testing and re-testing before becoming an "overnight sensation."

Some individuals and companies have generated millions of dollars by being or offering something unique, desirable or by meeting a need; others by attaching their reputations to something for which they were not known. In the latter cases, the name was clearly bigger than any of the products that carried it.

For many years "marketing," though a large umbrella term for a number of functions, was a line-item on the charts and budgets of mainstream businesses. "Image" was more of a concern of those in the often glamour-obsessed entertainment industry or the very proper office-seeker. But as the arts have become bigger business and increasingly both social and political considerations drive corporate decisions, the lines have narrowed and blurred.

The legal and medical professions have never been so publicly concerned about their "image." And rightly so. Some of the most high-profile lawyers and doctors, far from distinguishing themselves or their professions, are most noteworthy for their arrogance, opportunism, and periodic immersions in scandal. Academia, the arts, science, the military and even our churches are finding that their fortunes increasingly rise and fall based on polling data that speak to their "image."

A good image, nurtured, protected and brought to full bloom can create a halo that will light up the personality, the product, the company and the stock market.

Where is the line drawn between quality, value, talent and image? How much does the public really care?

Walt Disney, Ralph Lauren, Ted Turner, John Sculley, Ross Perot, Lee Iacocca and Martha Stewart are a few of the names of people who have learned to master *Image Marketing* for themselves and their companies. Others have tried with notable successes and failures.

But attaining and maintaining a good image can't be an end in itself. And a good image is not insurance against rough times ahead. But to cultivate a good image and maximize its inherent value, strengthens one's position should rough times hit. Of no small value as well is the support of those who have been customers, clients, users of products and supporters who feel "invested" enough to identify with a particular entity. Of such situations are good images perpetuated.

The ideas and recommendations in this book don't constitute a magic formula, but it is largely a formula nonetheless. Much of what is here grows from having an idea and a plan, believing in what you're doing and following through. Images are reflections of what people think. Our aim is to help you give them something to think about.

Image Marketing

The Rules

Perception vs. Reality

In our "highly enlightened" twentieth century, we learned that two people could indeed look at the same thing and see it quite differently. And, just as importantly, each person would go off and describe it to others as they saw it and those people would, in their own words, tell others and opinions would be formed.

Of such basic truths are untruths often born and reborn.

People's perceptions are based on what they know—or *think* they know. Based on these perceptions, people buy, sell, vote, travel, invest and make pretty much every major and minor decision that governs their lives and affects the lives of those around them.

It is true that perception and reality are often the same thing, but as wizards and marketers know, illusions can be created and words written to affect people's *perceptions of reality*.

For example, the President makes a speech and, within hours, a poll is released that says 75 percent of the people, many of whom actually *heard* the speech, think he is doing a good job. A week later, another poll is released that says 52 percent of people think the President is doing a good job. Different days, different samplings, perhaps even different demographics and control group size. Still, the news in the morning paper begins, "President's Approval Rating Plummets." The President's people will attempt to explain and their efforts will be described as "spin control." An impression will linger that the President is in trouble.

In another situation, a murder trial dominated the news for months and each night, based on reported highlights of the day in court, a high-tech sampling of opinions of travellers on the information superhighway told the world what percentage of the people "voting" thought the accused person guilty or innocent. The number fluctuated wildly from week to week as lawyers and witnesses performed for the cameras of Court TV and the Cable News Network. Perceptions here had consequences that literally involved life and death.

With respect to these two examples, we might all consider ourselves fortunate that elections aren't held weekly and that it's only the jury's vote that counts.

We are all governed by our perceptions of what we think we know, not necessarily what *is*. This fact has been exploited successfully and reported enough times to create a cloud of suspicion that hangs especially heavy over the heads of people who are trying to sell something, whether it's a product, a service or themselves.

KNOWING YOUR MARKET

No sane business traveller would arrive in another town without the proper business accessories, clothing, a confirmed hotel room, and a firm appointment to meet with clients or prospects. Yet, corporations regularly waste fortunes by launching products or changing products—or *not* changing products—in complete ignorance of the climate and size of the target market, let alone the basic *perceptions* of those who comprise it.

A wonderful line worth repeating often is there are those who listen and those who wait to talk. Research is about listening to the voice of your market.

Research has shown time and again that there is a direct correlation between a product's level of awareness and its market share. Even more fascinating is the fairly common *perception* that if a product is a *better known* product, it's a *better product.*

But is it? Or is it only more heavily advertised and more widely available, momentarily fashionable or more easily affordable?

Marketing consultants Al Ries and Jack Trout contend: "There are no best products. All that exist in the world of marketing are perceptions in the minds of the customer or prospect. The perception is the reality. Everything else is an illusion."

But how can that be? Can the tens of millions of dollars spent to advertise claims of superiority be only a costly ruse? What about all that laboratory testing and the opinions of nine-out-of-ten doctors and the conferring of "number one" status by the foremost such conferring authority?

One solidly definitive answer could lie in the old bromide "everything's relative." Just as the selection of last year's best movie is made from only those movies submitted for consideration and not from the larger group of every movie that was made during that year, businesses have their way of interpreting and presenting data that support their claims—and try to support the image the business seeks to create.

While the consultants' opinions may seem cynical or jaded, their conclusion on perceptions is certainly worth considering. The ultimate purchase decision may be made for a lot of different reasons and the determination of which product is "best" is in actuality a conclusion more often than not based on the individual or collective taste or some quantifiable standard, but *perception* will be based on information.

What then is perception and what is reality? The definitive answer to this time-honored question is that sometimes they are the same thing; sometimes they are not; and sometimes it's just hard to tell.

Consider, as the year 1994 drew to a close, the story in the *New York Times,* under the headline "Eating in 1995: The Year Beef Came Back." Without being reminded, readers knew that media coverage over several previous years had focused on the explosive sales of chicken, various kinds of fish, and even soybean-based versions of meat alternatives. This was a response to rising instances of heart disease, high cholesterol levels and conditions of poor health caused, in part, by diets high in fats, particularly fat from red meat. Maintaining a healthy diet had become fashionable. The *New York Times* story noted ". . . the bulk of the population is eating larger portions of nutrient-poor food and, consequently, obesity and health problems due to diet are rising."

Did this signify the workout tapes, health club memberships and organic vegetables that defined life in the 1980s were history? Not exactly. The same article offered in its subhead: "Fat is up, but so is low-fat. Organic foods are growing; pretzels are too. When it comes to vegetables, iceberg lettuce is still a favorite."

The net impression of the story seemed to be that unhealthy food sales were up, while healthy food sales were up as well. A little something for everybody. Maybe the real story is the passing of a fad period with consumers now taking advantage of a broad range of choices available to them, sometimes indulging themselves and sometimes choosing more moderate alternatives.

To marketers, this conclusion, if valid, might pose an interesting challenge: how to market during a period when one product or one way is not the obvious clear direction or choice, but *diversity* is the choice (if indeed there's any suggestion of a choice at all).

Historically marketers have looked for "trends" to guide budgeting and positioning decisions. Professionals, sensitive to the public *perception* of what's currently in fashion, may find this kind of situation to be one of those deadly gaps where there's no major dominant influence screaming to guide the market. At such times too, the new product introductions appear to be largely horizontal with brand extensions, line extensions and companion products to familiar names vastly outnumbering any new names in the field.

While the look of the marketplace may be more diverse, eclectic or operating at low volume, the basic rules for marketers remain unchanged. If customers, clients and prospects make their decisions based on *perceptions,* reliable market research remains the most valuable and essential ingredient in the marketer's bag.

Just as the public wants information about the product or service it's buying, the marketer needs to know, understand and consider the factors that influence those decisions. According to John Lytle, President of the consulting firm Elmhurst Management Service, "Two-thirds of this country's companies fail to satisfy superior needs because their perceptions of what their customers really want are far from reality."

While market research was particularly fashionable in the 1980s, the years that followed saw research budgets reduced along with most other budgets.

A major factor in reluctance to commit to market research is management ego. To collect information about what customers and prospects like and don't like about your own product and company, as well as that of your competition is frequently viewed by management as, perhaps, not just a bitter pill, but a sign of being out-of-touch with the market. Obviously, no one wants to admit to that, much less to be the one spending money to receive information that you think you already have—or that your Board thinks you already know. If this describes you, a word of advice: Get over it!

Not knowing unequivocally what factors are currently influencing your customers and prospects is simply not a justifiable position for a person in charge. The best doctors still know enough to take the patient's pulse at regular intervals. To learn what your public thinks of you, or how their opinions may have changed is extremely valuable information. Just as important is what your public thinks of your competitors and your industry and how *those* opinions may have changed.

If a decision to commit to market research is a problem for management or the Board, consider this advice attributed to Julia Child, who is said to have told would-be chefs: if the meal doesn't turn out the way it is supposed to, serve it anyway, just call it something else:

- Competitive intelligence
- Demographic study
- Customer satisfaction survey

Whatever. The point is to get it done.

Real research—learning how people perceive you, your company, product, service and competition, inside, outside and at the shareholder, regulator and media levels—is a real asset. Like any real asset, it requires an investment.

Additionally, research that is older than your married children is of questionable value to anyone but the company archivist. Change is inevitable, but changing times don't necessarily signify inherent dissatisfaction. Certainly your research can reveal good news, such as your public perceives you to be doing a wonderful job and vastly superior to your competition—even ahead of your industry. More than a few ad campaigns have been based on receiving great feedback from satisfied constituents. But had the research not been conducted to determine this, an element of doubt might have existed at some levels about how the public *really* perceived you and your products were performing. That doubt could have led to changes, real or cosmetic, that weren't needed and, in any case, were initiated for the wrong reasons.

Research may also reveal that you're doing everything right, but some segments of your public don't know that and, worse yet, may *perceive* quite the opposite of what is true.

For example, *Rolling Stone* magazine, which began publishing in 1968, had a long-running series of ads years later, usually two-page spreads, with the consistent headline "Perception. Reality." The left-hand page, under "Perception" usually showed a photograph of a flower child or a hippie or a young revolutionary in 1960s headband, peace symbol and torn jeans. On the right-hand page, under "Reality" was a photo of a bright, attractive, alert person of Baby Boomer or Generation X age (20s through 40s), dressed casually but well, sometimes pictured with a child.

It appeared that the message that came back from research was that the magazine was considered by potential advertisers as a reflection of the moment in time that marked its creation. The magazine wanted advertisers to know that it had *started* as something of an alternative or counter-culture publication, but had grown up along with its readers. It still loved art, pop culture and rock 'n' roll. It still wanted to provide a platform for outsiders' opinions. But just as so many of the people who made up "the Woodstock generation" went on to become teachers, artists, lawyers and accountants, the magazine that spoke to them and for them had also put on grown-up clothes, matured and even become a parent—spinning off other publications directed at both segmented and mainstream audiences.

Rolling Stone told its story to advertisers through ads that appeared on a consistent basis in trade publications, such as *Adweek, Advertising Age* and elsewhere. They pounded away at the "Perception. Reality." differences. Through public relations efforts, they publicized to newspaper columns, television and radio news shows, particular articles, interviews, profiles and investigative pieces that showed a mature and contemporary image. They published coffee table books on music and film and produced television specials that sought to position *Rolling Stone* as a hipper, more socially relevant chronicler of the times, personalities, music, literature and art. Presidential candidates would willingly be interviewed and appear on *Rolling Stone*'s cover, a recognition of its influence. That recognition was now being sought among advertisers.

Following the evolution of its audience and reflecting their lifestyle(s) helped to keep *Rolling Stone* profitable nearly three decades later. A key word here is "lifestyle(s)" as, like many good friends whose paths diverge, *Rolling Stone* core readers could be said to love the Grateful Dead, Simon and Garfunkel and the anti-war movement, but went on instead—or in addition—to embrace the work of a variety of jazz, country, new age, and classical performers as well as, in some corners, conservative politics.

Rolling Stone recognized that its continued existence depended on maintaining the loyalty of its core audience, despite its growing diversity, while exploiting its position as younger, hipper and more socially-conscious than, say *People* magazine or *The New Yorker*—two publications whose audience it sought.

The focus on *lifestyles* in marketing is a more important factor than just identifying demographics and target markets. An analytical perspective on lifestyles will provide a great deal of information on *perceptions* or *images*.

Often a customer, client or prospect will not so much *have* a particular lifestyle as he or she will *aspire* to have it.

Consider the successful advertising campaigns that have asked the question, "Can you see yourself in this picture?" On a beach, at the club, at the wheel, in control. . . .

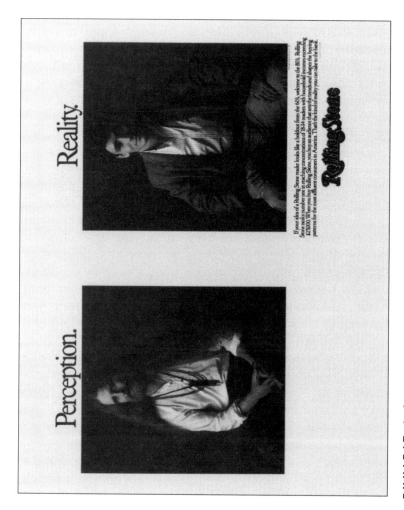

EXHIBIT 1.1

Rolling Stone

This ad from a long-running series for *Rolling Stone* magazine spoke directly to the issue of perception vs. reality.

Recognizing aspirations has long been a key to marketing programs. Imagery is a pivotal component of these programs.

The ad headlines "What becomes a legend most?" to sell furs or "What sort of man reads *Playboy*?" show lifestyles suggesting glamour, power and privilege. They appeal to aspirations. They also address *image* on two levels: the image of the product in the ad and the subliminal, subconscious, secret or even overt desire of the consumer to be the person in the ad, to adopt the image, live the dream. People at the broadest range of socio-economic levels are susceptible to this.

Marketers need to be aware of research that not only determines the market's opinions of the product, service company, industry and competition in terms of price, packaging, integrity and quality, but they need to know who these people are who make up the market. Are they male, female, both, young, old, ethnic, conservative, more cost-conscious than quality-conscious or vice versa? Do they have a sense of humor? Do they have a history of recommending what they choose to others or do they prefer the idea of being the only ones in their circle to have and do what they have and do?

Getting the critical perceptions on what you are offering is only half the research. Knowing all you can learn about the hot buttons—the motivating factors—that drive the people who make up your market is just as important.

In 1994, *Advertising Age* said about lifestyles, "The consumer of the '90s is a new and different breed. Frugal and savvy, shoppers have adopted a 'casual living' approach to everything from apparel to fitness to dining . . . yet, faced with a radical shift in the U.S. family structure and lingering concerns about the economy and jobs, consumers' desires for spirituality and hope are stronger than ever."

If the *Advertising Age* research referenced here is valid, using such words to describe consumers in the 1990s as frugal, savvy, concerned and spiritual, it is inconceivable that anyone going into the marketing arena in the 1990s wouldn't want to know that and somehow reflect any and all of the characteristics in their planning.

CREATING PERCEPTION

This isn't rocket science. Before you can *market* an image, you must *have* an image. You must identify your target market and let them know who you are and what you do and why they should care. Your image is the reflection of people's perceptions.

If the image of you that people take away is based on their perception of you and their perception is based upon what they know of you, it's important that you manage and control that flow of information about you to the greatest degree possible. But most important is that there *be* information; that you create a stream of information to raise awareness.

How that is done is a process only as complex as you allow it to become. The White House Press Secretary used to be the media contact who disseminated statements and copies of speeches and got answers to the reporters' questions. It was a simple enough system and a fairly efficient one. In the modern White House, the Press Secretary has any number of assistants, not to mention sort of sharing the job with a Communications Director and several personal advisors and assistants to the President and the First Lady . . . and *their* assistants. Increasingly, the place began to look and function somewhat like the Post Office or a ball team on which everyone is playing third base.

Business, alas, in dealing with the media and public seems to have taken on the characteristics of this model. Everyone seems to want to be in charge of controlling the flow of information, but no one seems to actually want to take responsibility for what is said. So, not much is said that seems very substantive. Within this framework, reporters, editors, columnists or producers collect information on business wherever they can. That includes calling competitors, former employees, former partners or retired regulators or executives or anyone who has played golf or tennis or had lunch with a current or former executive of the business during the last eleven years. If that seems an exaggeration, it is only slightly so. Even the media with the highest sense of integrity is not above receiving news from a source you might consider less than credible or as having a personal axe to grind.

The person who says "I'll let my record speak for itself" or "I'm not going to dignify those remarks with a comment" may as well be wearing a large "kick me!" sign. Responses such as those used to be considered satisfactory, even dignified, but enough people have hidden behind them over the years as to render them empty. Remember that your goal is to control the flow of information about you and to do that you must *provide* information that clearly defines you. If you don't, someone else will and the odds that it will be someone who wishes you great success are not in your favor.

The next chapter will focus more specifically on different avenues of communication available to you—and they are many. Each of them has its own rules, rather like those private clubs, where members take themselves and what they do seriously. They should. Receiving, collecting and disseminating information to a variety of audiences is what they do and if you want to reach their audience, you accede to their rules. You can still, however, have certain degrees of control and even make friends along the way once you've decided:

- **Consider the type of an image you want to present.**

- **Initiate the contact.** Waiting to be called is flattering, but taking the initiative allows you to, in effect, play "host" and introduce the subjects rather than having to try to fit what you want known into a discussion someone else may have initiated for wholly other purposes.

- **Be forthcoming.** Yours isn't the only valuable time. Respect that people have their schedules and agenda and get to the point.

- **Don't overstate your case** so that your interviewer finds it hard to believe. A little exaggeration or bragging is usually expected, but the person who keeps insisting "everyone went crazy, fell off their chairs; they couldn't believe how great this was" rarely convinces anyone that the audience's enthusiasm was quite so unrestrained. And that doesn't help them frame your story.

- **Don't wear out your welcome.** Just as the rule holds that you don't talk too loud or too long, follow-up calls and faxes can be annoying. Someone you are trying to influence favorably should not think of you as a pest or someone who does not respect other people's time. A conversation followed by a thank you note that says to call if more information is needed, usually is adequate.

- **Use subtlety.** That your public should become effectively aware of you, your company, your product, service or message should occur on several levels. Creating a good and lasting image in someone's mind rarely begins with an explosion, but rather with an announcement. Whether the announcement is made directly to the general public, the media or a specific target group, take it easy. Public relations, advertising and collaterals, if appropriate, will all get their turn at bat—their time to do their part of the job. But to initially create perceptions—awareness of you—don't give more information than people can recall or digest at one time. To make what you have to say more memorable, think of the adage "less is more." The broadcast media is frequently accused of reporting news through "soundbites," very short, usually colorful comments. But that's what people remember, not the lengthy dissertations.

- **Identify and use your tools.** Know which delivery system works best for the message that will generate an awareness of you and enhance your image. Your overall strategy may include an advertising or public relations agency simply handling everything. But some editors, reporters, producers or other persons of influence remember the person who picked up the phone and called. Others like to receive personal letters or invitations to meet, perhaps over a meal. The manner in which you reach out to those you hope to influence and from whom you want support, whether it's a full-page newspaper ad or a personal note or an invitation to coffee or a skywriter's message, should be consistent with the type of image you are seeking to create. Recall the times you have heard or read that something was "discussed over lunch at the Russian Tea Room" or someone "met in his suite at The Four Seasons." The location itself suggests an image you then associate with the participants. Typically, entertainers don't announce major career plans from a room at a budget motor lodge and CEOs don't try to influence securities analysts or the editors of *The Wall Street Journal* by speaking to them from a pay telephone at a fast-food restaurant. A note on museum postcards or personalized stationery, a gift basket of fresh fruit or flowers, a call from a plane, a limo or another city conveys a particular image of the person initiating the contact as caring enough to be attentive.

MAINTAINING PERCEPTIONS

Apart from ongoing advertising and public relations programs, assume you've succeeded in generating public goodwill and the perception that your efforts are well-placed. You may not feel you've quite got the world by the tail, but you feel you've "made it."

Now what? Few individuals ever succeeded and simply closed the curtains while the theme music played. There's always the next day, the next market cycle and the next challenge.

More than a few families have experienced the financial pressure of "keeping up appearances," trying to maintain an image of prosperity, even when long-term forecasts are a little unstable. Good judgement at such times says "live within your means." Reality is that a half-century of credit buying and time-payment plans have encouraged and allowed people at virtually all income levels to maintain a higher standard of living than they can pay for today.

Business usually finds itself in the same situation. When all is going well, there is invariably a cacophony of voices shouting to cut the marketing and advertising budgets because it's not needed as much anymore. The marketing department wants more so it can take advantage of the good times and be in a stronger position should bad times be ahead. In tough times, one side wants to cut the marketing budget because budget-cutting is prudent, while the other side pleads that a cut would hurt their image in a cutthroat competitive environment.

It seems awfully simplistic to suggest that operating budgets, including marketing, should just be what they need to be to get the job done. Overindulgence is never good business, nor is trying to maintain the image of being a successful operation without the necessary funding.

The list of recommendations presented here was preceded by the words "consider the type of image you want to present." A basic requirement must be that the image also reflects who and what you are. It's true that the right spin or slant can help good look better or make bad look *not so bad,* but the process can't make something what it is not. If a business or individual is struggling, there are ways to represent that positively and honestly: the underdog, the fighter, the try-harder factor. Keeping up appearances doesn't mean saying or even suggesting a concern is decidedly other than what it is.

When the suggestion is to "consider the type of image you want to present," one can assume the image chosen will not be a negative one. But it must also be a realistic one. If your enterprise is and remains successful, it should not be difficult to exploit that in all the best possible ways. If your image is not successful, go back to your research and examine what your public has to say about you. Then determine what you will have to do to make things right. Such corrective measures may be the very basis of your creating and maintaining a better public image.

It is fair to say that most entities that have successfully created an image in which they are perceived favorably by the public, maintain such perceptions by continuing to do what has worked for them, such as:

- Long-term sponsorship of annual or regularly scheduled events
- Support of local activities and teams or events
- Participation in charitable, scholastic or social programs
- Food drives

- Blood drives
- Toys-for-tots collection programs
- Support or participation in environmental programs

The list could go on and on. If your image is the reflection of how you are perceived, doing the basic public and community good works—and publicizing that fact—will take you a long way.

CHANGING PERCEPTIONS

Again, consider the type of image you want to present. If you are aware through research, or more obvious means, that your image is significantly different from what you want it to be, determine what must be done, or can be done, to change this.

Perhaps you are, or at least believe yourself to be, superior to your competition, but that does not seem obvious to your public. Why?

Do you advertise?

Does your competition advertise?

If the answer to both questions is yes, what are the advertising budget differences among competitors, the choices of media used and the tone or focus of the ads? Is there a clear correlation between the category leader and the suggestion that something is clearly "more correct" in one or more of these areas?

What are the competitors doing that you are not?

Check comparisons of price, service and length of time in business in the market.

Do you run the kind of advertising or marketing program that regularly identifies your competitors by name and makes direct comparisons?

Are your public suggestions of superiority heavy (or even tinged) with either arrogance or defensiveness?

Attitude and awareness research should tell you things you are doing wrong, if any.

But if your product or service is good and the market for it is good, one question you may have to address with regard to changing people's perception of you might have to do with changing *you*.

Without wanting to hurt anyone's feelings, a simple truth is there are certain personality traits that others find to be a turn-off. In business situations, one must consider seriously what, if anything, must be done.

There are people who absolutely will not stay at a particular hotel (or any in a chain) because of an immense dislike for the outspoken owner of the chain, who enjoys making public appearances—and in so doing says things people find to be offensive.

Some people will not buy books or go to movies produced by companies owned by a very public, high-profile figure whose methods of doing business offend them.

For every Charles Schwab, whose personality and apparent sincerity attract business, there is a CEO or personality who keeps people away. If this is your problem, recognize that a business should be more important than an executive ego. Simply put, if you don't have the right personality for the spokesperson job, stop walking the beat and take a desk job. If your diminished public role corresponds to an increase in business, learn from it. Of course, if you are the marketing person who has to break the news to an ego-heavy CEO that his or her public appearances are hurting business (and your kids are still in school and you don't have the next job lined up), consider again the immeasurable value of your independent market research report. An objective outsider's written conclusions and recommendations, left on the boss's desk, can put a bit of distance between you and the word.

On a less egocentric level, some people won't do business with a company they perceive as being not service oriented enough. How do you change their minds?

Bennigan's restaurants responded to complaints that service was slow by putting a stop watch on every table and promising if the meal wasn't delivered in fifteen minutes, it was free. It was a successful approach, helped perhaps by the fact that the food only had to go from kitchen to table. When Domino's Pizza tried a similar approach, delivering pizzas from restaurants to homes in a certain time frame, the jump in auto accidents and speeding tickets made the program a dangerous embarrassment. A better approach for Domino's might have been to offer some kind of enhancement that made the order, if late, worth waiting for. Sometimes, a simple apology in advance works wonders. Telling callers you are very busy, running behind schedule and appreciate their patience, is usually a very acceptable response. Again and again, courtesy—or a lack of courtesy—is cited as a chief complaint in consumer research. Remembering to say "thank you" and apologizing for delays and errors keeps people coming back because they feel their business is appreciated.

Another key complaint, besides a lack of courtesy, is the tendency to move away from the old department store credo that held "the customer is always right." Modern business appears to have a tendency to respond argumentatively—if at all—to customer complaints. Blaming computers, keeping callers "on hold," offering no explanation—much less an apology—for delays or mistakes, makes people angry. Compounding the situation will be promises from marketers and advertisers that "Service is our number one product" or "You're important to us" or "Your satisfaction is guaranteed" with a visible lack of follow-through from the service people. This may be the result of poor training (or *no* training), poor supervision, poor quality control or merely bad manners. None of these is good for business.

Start with a mission statement. Have everyone read it and sign it and follow through on it.

It's absurd to spend millions on advertising that promises a 10-minute oil change and then have the customer not even get someone from your company on the phone for that amount of time. Or once there, to find that the oil change takes 10 minutes after you've waited in line for a half-day.

In no area of your operation is research more important than when it comes to changing people's perceptions of you. You must very often *ask* people if you care and want to know what they think of you and, perhaps more importantly, what they would have you change.

And, then, *do* something with the information you receive. Don't ask people for comments and then argue with them and expect their goodwill. Just as it is said that the best type of advertising is word-of-mouth advertising, people who have a single upsetting experience, whether the result of an oversight, an error or a discourtesy, will tell people about it. Usually, a *lot* of people. But the opposite is true as well. Courtesy and honest, friendly service get talked about as well. This point seems blatantly simple, yet it usually triggers the highest level of surprise and forehead slapping.

Changing perceptions usually starts with changing the way you do things that are not getting results. Perhaps it's changing your ads, spokespeople, policies or personnel.

Businesses often spend large amounts to redecorate a location or update a logo or signage to appear fresh and contemporary. A new sign and a coat of paint won't help a business or a person who is more familiar and talked about for having a bad policy or a bad attitude. Use attitude and awareness research to guide you in what needs to be changed. An outside agency or consultant can help tell you *how* to change something, but it is your customers, clients and other involved members of your community or circle who must help you learn *what* needs to be done.

The first step in changing perceptions then is *listening.*

The second step is turning your listening into a workable plan. Too many people confuse being "reactive" with being "aggressive." Having and following a plan is the most efficient method of coordinating and measuring ongoing activity, as well as success. It's also common sense.

Not necessarily a "step," but an important component to your changing public perceptions is *patience,* a word most marketers hate because it seems almost a contradiction of the do-it-now(!) personality that is typical of successful marketers. In this high-tech era of instant communication, a reputation might have been damaged by a single scandal, story or interview, and of course you have to do something about that, but don't confuse the process of changing public perceptions, of image building, with "damage control" or "crisis management." They are not the same process. Whether a single constituent group or the entire universe has come to hold negative perceptions of you or your company or service based on a single "instant" event or slowly over time, the process of changing perceptions, of changing people's minds, short of hypnosis, takes time. Particularly, if you are attempting to change perceptions after a crisis situation, expect your public, under the best of circumstances to be especially cynical or suspicious. Your efforts to win them over must be both sincere and appear so. At times such as this, having and advancing a long term plan that suggests your commitment to stay the distance, as well as inviting people to check how you are doing at given intervals can be a useful part of building credibility, integrity and changing your critics' minds about you.

The long list of "comebacks" or successful turnaround stories have taught us that the public seems inherently to want to be fair. Getting another chance is much more the rule than the exception. The opportunity is there; the responsibility not to disappoint is great.

AT A GLANCE: THE RULES

1. People's perceptions are based on what they know—or what they think they know.
2. Market research is critical to determining the perceptions of the market. It means listening to your market.
3. There is a direct correlation between level of awareness and marketshare.
4. The public wants information about what it is buying and who's doing the selling; the marketer needs to know as much as possible about the tastes, trends and motivating factors of the public.
5. Determine what people at all levels within your company or organization think about your company, product or service and correlate that data with consumer marketshare.
6. Customers, clients or prospects don't always *have* a particular lifestyle as much as they might *aspire* to have it.
7. Recognize that market research is likely to reveal a diversity of choices and sentiments that may appear to be contradictory.

8. In order to create perceptions, there must be a steady flow of information to raise levels of public and industry awareness.

9. Keeping up a steady flow of information increases your chances of influencing what people think of you, your product, service or company. The absence of such information leaves it for your critics and competitors to define you.

10. Initiate contacts with the media, rather than hoping, demanding or waiting to be called. This heightens your likelihood of being able to influence the tone of the conversation.

11. Be forthcoming. Respect other people's time. By being direct and offering substantive information, you reduce the chances of being defined by your silence or someone else's interpretation of your position.

12. Don't overstate your case. A little exaggeration is expected, but outrageous claims, opinions and hype— however colorful—serve to haunt and embarrass over the long run.

13. Don't wear out your welcome. Maintaining a steady flow of information *means* information. The pesky follow-up calls and faxes become highly counterproductive when they don't offer anything new.

14. Use subtlety. Give the important details of your story to media, customers and prospects and leave the color for them to determine based on their own conclusions.

15. Resist the temptation to reduce the budget for marketing when things are good. Increase your resistance when times are bad. Your need to cultivate support and goodwill is not permanently achieved by the occasional, or even series of, successes.

16. Develop a marketing plan and stick to it.

17. Don't confuse *reacting* with being aggressive.

18. Your public's positive perceptions of you are frequently a reflection of reports of your good works in the community.

19. Regularly reevaluate your advertising and public relations efforts to be sure they are consistent with your overall marketing goals and not just sales.

20. Make certain that you have a Mission Statement, that all employees read and sign it and that it addresses maintaining a level of customer service and satisfaction that will help define and maintain your public image.

21. Be patient. Solid reputations are rarely made, maintained or changed for the better "instantly."

CHAPTER 2

The Tools

What People Think of You vs. *How* People Think of You

The value of *image* can't be overstated.

This book is about marketing, not a social commentary. Yet, an observation must be offered because of its relevance to the subject of marketing, particularly with regard to "images."

A strange phenomenon has taken place in recent years. Despite the significant influence of religion on society over the past several centuries, and the wording of the portion of the law which cites the presumption of innocence until proven guilty, the mood of the country has held otherwise. Anyone appears to be able to accuse anyone else of virtually anything and, if not get a day in court, get a press conference and coverage by usually respectable media. Since about 1990, the public has seemed ready or at least willing to entertain suggestions that successful enterprises were suspect until proven otherwise.

Creating and maintaining a good public image in an atmosphere of societal cynicism and suspicion become even more challenging. Still, the rewards to those who achieve public acceptance justify the efforts expended in meeting the challenge.

To reach a level of public awareness where the impact of your image is felt takes time, financial backing and a plan. It is true that there is the occasional "overnight success," who with a single television or print profile becomes the focus of tremendous attention. It is more often true that most overnight success stories involve considerable time and money put into test markets, trial runs and stints in the "minor leagues" before gaining that "instant" success. Those who didn't follow such a path very often find a lack of stability—or *legs*—to sustain success and end up with fifteen minutes of fame before returning to obscurity.

THE AVENUES OF AWARENESS

Marketers know that the term *marketing* itself has come to mean different things over the years. It has evolved into an umbrella under which packaging, positioning, pricing, promotion, distribution, sales, advertising, public relations and perhaps even research may fall. Most all of these individual areas of activity have any number of subcategories themselves.

For the purpose of an examination of the process of *image marketing,* the focus here might be limited to just those specific areas designated as *primary avenues of awareness*—advertising and public relations. While all other related functions clearly have an interrelated role to play and budgets will frequently intersect and overlap, it is basically advertising and PR that provide marketers the processes to create, influence, and maintain public perceptions. Both areas then become themselves somewhat umbrella terms.

Advertising is a "catch-all" phrase. Consider:

- corporate advertising/institutional advertising
- image advertising
- product advertising
- co-op advertising
- promotion advertising

EXHIBIT 2.1

SunGard

An elevator panel is the image of simplicity in describing a highly advanced financial record-keeping software system from SunGard.

Public relations, very often dismissed (even by advertising agencies and ad professionals) as simply a publicity function, encompasses a good deal more, such as:

- customer or client relations
- employee relations
- event management
- governmental relations
- media and press relations
- member relations
- publications
- research management
- shareholder relations/financial relations
- speech writing

Not every individual, company or service will need every discipline or function, but knowing the value and differences of each is important. Maximizing visibility to the analyst community to enhance the value of the stock price is hardly the same program as event management or governmental relations. An ad might have some benefit to a community relations effort and a newsletter or speech might impress the Board of Directors or members of a trade association, but the age of "one size fits all" has not yet arrived when it comes to structuring an effective marketing program.

ADVERTISING

In *Getting the Best from Your Ad Agency,* I provided a nine-point checklist that represented an overview of an effective advertising program. The points emphasize the importance of market research and a marketing plan. An abridged version of that list offers these recommendations:

1. **Define the market.** It's fine to think of your message as being for all the world to hear, but your target customer, prospect or constituent group is likely

somewhat narrower than that. Know your prospective audience in terms of age, sex, marital and family status; income; business/profession; geographic influence.

2. **Define your competition.**
3. **Prepare a competitive analysis.**
4. **Create a profile of your customer** including how much your customer knows about you—alone and relative to your competition—and key considerations of those things your customer considers important (cost, guarantee, years in business, location, cleanliness, timeliness . . .).
5. **Identify key sources of information** about you, your product or service.
6. **Know why your business gets better or worse—** seasonality, discounts, advertising, rebates, news stories.
7. **Know exactly what you want your advertising to accomplish,** such as increase awareness, reverse a negative image, expand markets, or increase sales or marketshare.
8. **Merchandise your research.** The real value of information lies in both *how* and *that* you can use it.
9. **Establish benchmarks for results.** Critics of market research sometime say that a survey or a study can be created to determine whatever it is the client wants to conclude. This is on the same level as the Evil Queen demanding the mirror tell her she is the fairest in the land. The point of research is to either validate what you are doing or guide you through the process of correcting what can or needs to be corrected. And *doing* it.

Corporate advertising, also often described as *institutional advertising,* aims at helping you, your product or service become a better known *name.* Its purpose is to raise awareness and recognition. Rarely is a product mentioned in a corporate ad, unless the product is so important and well-regarded as to create a halo effect that reflects favorably on the corporation, such as a bold, yet discreet, line like "makers of . . . (insert well-known product here)."

The primary purpose of corporate advertising is to promote greater awareness of the company to the investment community— investment advisors, securities analysts, stockholders, bankers and fund managers. The product is far less relevant here than promoting the efficiency of the management and the company's financial performance. Basically, the objective is to position a company as being on the leading edge of the industry, or the market in general, and the company's management as the leaders within. Corporate advertising is specifically used with the objective of seeing *that* people think of you. Some examples of familiar corporate ads or themes include:

- You can be sure if its Westinghouse
- Grace: One Step Ahead of a Changing World
- Toshiba: In touch with tomorrow
- DuPont: Better things for better living through chemistry
- GE: Progress is our most important product
- GE (again): We bring good things to life
- Ford: Quality is job one.

Image advertising is intended to influence *how* people think of you. Again, the product in the ads is of secondary importance. The main thing is to show how much happier everyone will be and how the quality of life will improve thanks to this product, company or entity. It is typically represented in the "can you see yourself in this picture?" kind of imagery, whether on TV, in print or in outdoor ads. Mood and lifestyle are important elements in image ads.

Some marketers who take pride in having a singular, sales-oriented focus tend to dismiss image ads as a lot of calendar art and touchy-feely messages that will make you laugh or make you cry but won't make you buy product. Others, who grudgingly concede that image ads can in fact make people feel good enough about a company to invest in it, buy its products or services and support it, but they contend nonetheless that it simply takes too long for its impact to be felt.

Those who are bottom-line oriented lament that the effects of image ads are subjective and long-term, thus making the measure of the ads' effectiveness difficult or impossible to determine. Proponents of the form point out that coupons, discounts or promoting will get the public to sample, but long-term brand loyalty is based, more than most factors, on image—how the public *feels* about what you're offering. Some memorable examples of image ads that left the marketplace in a particularly good mood are:

- Bell System: Reach out and touch someone
- Eastman Kodak: For the times of your life
- State Farm: Like a good neighbor, State Farm is there
- U.S. Army: Be all that you can be
- Nike: Just do it!
- United Negro College Fund: A mind is a terrible thing to waste
- Motel 6: We'll leave the light on for you
- Pepperidge Farm remembers
- Virginia Slims: You've come a long way, baby.

Very occasionally, a corporate and an image message can be embodied in a single line or message that leaves a lasting impression such as:

- The GM Mark of Excellence
- Zenith, the quality goes in before the name goes on
- Fly the friendly skies of United

Product advertising is the least difficult type of advertising to understand, yet the most difficult to produce successfully on a long-term basis. The product ad is a straightforward statement of the product's qualities, benefits and, hopefully, unique characteristics. It is a simple message: here's who and what we are and why you should buy what we're offering. But the product ads, with their lack of subtlety, are the greatest in number and therefore constitute the largest part of the dreaded "advertising clutter," the "glut" of ads with the largest "tune-out" factor. What are termed *retail* ads in newspapers are run by local or national retailers who by usually offering specials or sales, are seeking an immediate response. They are almost exclusively product ads.

These ads also have the fastest response and most rapid instances of diminishing returns. That is, their subject is timely. Additionally, they quickly become the ads people remember that they have already seen or heard, and therefore tune-out after fewer viewings than other ads. Usually humor, sex, music or a celebrity will help distinguish one product ad from another, but creativity, the hallmark of effective corporate and image ads, is most needed in product ads and usually is secondary to an aggressive or blatant product pitch, call-to-action, and the tendency to try putting 60 seconds of advertising into a 30-second spot. Nonetheless, some great product ads have included messages people have long remembered, such as:

- Campbell soups are Mmm, Mmm good!
- Hallmark—when you care enough to send the very best
- You're in good hands with Allstate
- This Bud's for you
- Things go better with Coke.

Co-op advertising can be—and often is—quite simply a little bit of everything thrown into one ad and very often quite good. In a co-op ad program, a manufacturer, producer or other preeminent entity creates an ad that emphasizes brand quality and uniqueness and pays all or most of the cost for the ad to run locally with space or time allocated for a "local tag" or some regional customizing. In some cases, this is the largest amount or the *only* amount of advertising that certain local retailers will be able to run. A very small player has the opportunity to put his, her or a company's name, address and phone number on ads that have likely been created by some of the top creative agencies in advertising. It may not include exactly the message or visuals every local participant would have chosen, but it does include elements of carefully crafted effective advertising.

Options give you investment options— and 52,000 callers have discovered a new one— absolutely Free!

A Free videotape, options guide and options disclosure document. 52,000 calls have come in from individual investors and financial professionals for these insights into the Options Tool. Thousands are now learning about all the various options that only options can give them—from hammering down investment security to prying up new profits. After looking at these materials, many have used options for the first time. And among those who were already using options, a number are now putting them to work for their portfolios even more! Although options involve risk and are not suitable for everyone, if you want to discover the options of stock options—and for Free—call now!

Call now for your Free videotape "The Options Tool— Understanding Stock Options," options guide and options disclosure document. 1-800-952-TOOL

The Options Industry Council

American Stock Exchange
Chicago Board Options Exchange
New York Stock Exchange
Pacific Stock Exchange
Philadelphia Stock Exchange
The Options Clearing Corporation

EXHIBIT 2.2

The Options Industry Council
Trading options is perceived by investors as highly sophisticated, complex and technical. This ad describes in a single picture and very few words how options fit into an investment program. It was prepared by five securities exchanges and their trade clearing corporation, presenting a common interest in education at The Options Industry Council.

Historically, some marketers dismiss or look down on co-op advertising. This is usually a reflection of their feelings over having had no influence over the creative components of the ad and the fact that customization or insertion of a tag must be done under certain, sometimes very restrictive, conditions to qualify for co-op funding. This is unfortunate because some of the creative work is quite good and should not be ignored because of a marketing director's ego. Having said that, it is equally important to be sensitive to the tone, look and feeling of a co-op ad in the event its representations are inconsistent with the "image" objectives of a particular local marketing plan. To run the ad for the exposure, simply because someone else is paying for it, can be counter-productive. When going for an image, if a co-op ad doesn't help, pass on it, at any price and stick with your plan.

Promotional support in advertising typically means ads created and placed to support an event, concert, sweepstakes, celebrity appearance or anything outside the parameters and goals of the annual ad budget. To fragment an ad budget by requiring it to support a promotion rather than promote a product, company or image is the worst kind of dilution of resources. These ads are forgotten shortly after being seen, much less once the promotion ends. Ads of virtually every type—product, corporate or image—should have recall value to be at all effective. Promotions themselves, much less their ads, have no significant recall once the promotion ends. The exception to this is a souvenir program or a specific commemorative keepsake, such as posters or t-shirts.

EVALUATING EFFECTIVENESS

Even the most experienced professionals differ over which type of advertising is the most effective. The fact is, of course, the most effective form is the one that works best for you, and that is determined by which form best responds to the dictates of your marketing plan.

Some persons or companies have single-page marketing plans that are virtual checklists of what to do and how to do it. Others have voluminous documents developed by consultants or MBAs with contingencies for every occurrence. There are books written specifically on the subject of writing a marketing plan. Again, the one that meets your needs is the right one for you.

The fairly standard elements of an effective marketing plan include these points:

1. situation analysis
2. objectives
3. strategy and tactics
4. timeline
5. budget

A competent consultant or agency should be able to prepare (or help prepare) an effective situation analysis and should have recommendations for a strategy and tactics to achieve the objective in the stated time frame and within budget. A consultant or agency should also be able to identify when the objective, time frame or budget are unrealistic and where reconsideration or revisions might be appropriate. Once such a marketing plan is fixed, the right advertising format and campaign can be developed.

A corporate advertising campaign is appropriate if the business needs to reassure stockholders or lenders or shore-up employee spirits. Product advertising is the statement of ongoing presence in the marketplace of your product or service and is important to build and maintain market share. It is the simple principle of out-of-sight, out-of-mind. If the competitors' products are advertised and yours are not, the competitors will achieve greater market share. It's that simple.

Image advertising is basically the choice for all occasions. In addition to or instead of product ads, an image message creates a "feel good" sense that creates or promotes interest and loyalty and leaves a more lasting impression than most other forms of advertising. Image ads, as previously noted, should have little or no emphasis on products. Product ads, on the other hand, should reflect the image you want to present as well as the product and, at the very least, close with a slogan or phrase that suggests your mission statement or your uniqueness in the marketplace—something that sets you apart from competitors.

In a *Wall Street Journal* promotional piece titled "7 Steps to Improving Your Corporate Image," adman James R. Gregory notes: "Whatever other purpose an image campaign may have, such advertising almost always helps prepare the marketplace for the sale of the product."

In *The Image-Makers—Power and Persuasion on Madison Avenue,* William Meyers writes, "Chevrolet, for example, has sold hundreds of thousands of Camaros . . . by positioning the vehicle as the coolest car on the market. Dr. Pepper became a major soft drink in this country with its 'Be a Pepper' campaign, which offered teenagers the reassurance of group acceptance and friendship."

The image and the product can each reinforce the value of the other.

Image advertising also includes the area "advocacy advertising" or "cause advertising." The American Association of Advertising Agencies defines advocacy advertising as

> advertising paid for by a corporation and designed to communicate the company's position on public issues which have some connection with its business activities. This definition would include, at one end of the spectrum, statements of position on pending legislation. It would exclude, at the other end, product advertising or corporate "goodwill" advertising aimed at corporate name or product recognition.

With all due respect to the AAAA, that's a pretty tall order and not always on target. For example, the Mobil Oil Company's series of "advertorials" has been running in many major newspapers with some consistency since about 1970. The focus of these ads—rarely illustrated, direct, usually political in nature—is indeed "designed to communicate the company's position on public issues which have some connection with its business activities." But they also, through the same ad vehicle, seek to promote "corporate goodwill . . . aimed at corporate name or product recognition." And it seems to work just fine. Mobil's image is consistently more than that of a "fat cat oil company," a designation typically applied to giants in its industry.

So often the benefit of advocacy advertising is far more subtle, a step or two from what were once public service announcements.

The Partnership for a Drug-Free America's "Say no to drugs" campaign uses various celebrities issuing warnings and anti-drug messages. NBC Television regularly runs commercial spots, which they themselves underwrite and produce on behalf of various social causes. The AIDS awareness effort operates much the same way. None of these issues could be said to have anything much directly to do with its sponsor.

Advocacy advertising—the taking of a position with respect to a particular issue or cause—carries the same type of risks and rewards as other types of "investment." Those who choose advocacy should understand that in doing so, they are going out on a limb—and a very visible limb at that—by taking a potentially unpopular stand that may very well offend or upset some people and cost some business. On the other hand, it may at the same time generate new respect from segments of the market that had taken no notice of the company before. It is a bold move that could be great or disastrous.

The terms *corporate* and *image advertising* are, on occasion, used interchangeably or as *corporate image marketing*. A person using that term most likely means "corporate" advertising.

PUBLIC RELATIONS

If you start with a surface that has nothing in it or on it that will cause it to shine, it won't matter how much you rub or polish it. It still won't shine. PR is a lot the same way. There are people who will toss around expressions like "he needs to get some PR" or "that company really needs to do something about its PR," when what they really mean is that *he* or *the company* has a poor image and needs to do something about *that*.

The first thing he or it needs to do is to "be good" or "get good." The second thing is to understand what public relations can and can't do. There is no amount of "PR" that can turn something that is substantively bad into something good.

It is true that you can fool some of the people all of the time and all of the people some of the time, but eventually, the news and tabloid press will come around during sweeps week and set things straight.

What PR efforts frequently achieve that make people think that PR can make bad look good is that a competent public relations professional will look for—and usually find—something good to say about anyone or anything.

With experience over more than three decades in the field, Philip Lesly, president of The Philip Lesly Company, offered that

> Public relations started as publicity—now just one of its phases—because, as it became harder for people with different backgrounds to understand and know about each other, the first necessity was for one group to tell the others about itself. In developing, public relations has come to include a great many other functions besides telling about someone or some group. It also tells the group about what others think of it; it helps the group determine what it must do to get the goodwill of others; it plans ways and means of winning that goodwill; and it carries on activities designed to win it.

Telling others about one's self is the essence of publicity. How one tells the story will determine the success or failure of the aim to win the community's goodwill, to create perceptions, to build an *image.*

For years an old adage held, "I don't care what you write about me, just spell my name right." One can only wonder what sort of mentality truly believes "any publicity is good publicity." Certainly, not anyone who counts on the goodwill of others to support a career or a business. The concept of "spin control"—putting the best face on a story—certainly does not presuppose that *any* publicity is good publicity. Indeed, some entrepreneurs, investors and others pay press agents to help keep them *out* of the public eye.

But noting the various phases, areas and subcategories that might be considered under the "PR" umbrella, to create awareness and shape an image, it is necessary to go to the marketing plan. Just as corporate, product and image advertising each have their uses and applications, public relations is not a one-size-fits-all-situations proposition. You have various identifiable "publics."

Per your marketing plan, prepare your situation analysis, objectives, strategy and tactics, time line and budget. Determine, too, the target or targets of your efforts. Who do you need or want to reach? Who has a particular value to you in having an ability or an opportunity to influence the target audience you want to reach? Your "publics" include any customers, clients, stockholders, members, regulators or legislators, investors, the media, employees, underwriters or others in your industry or profession.

Of various alternative approaches available to you, choose that which seems best suited to your objective. Don't overreach. If what you hope to accomplish is an internal matter, going to the general media might be a waste of effort and resources. If you want to reach the investment community, procedures and media differ from those that might be employed to publicize or support an event or cause. That may seem obvious, but a term that comes up with increasing frequency among professionals is *waste*—paying to reach an audience with little or no interest in a given subject. With the proliferation of "new media" in the 1990s—cable television channels, videos and alternative publications, as well as software and interactive media—comes the increased opportunity to make wrong choices.

Customer or *client relations* is directed largely to keeping business—a satisfied clientele—and to creating and preserving a perception that service is assumed. Surveys of your constituents' opinions on a list of subjects, including the quality of your service not only contributes information to your research data base but sends those constituents a message of your concern. Hot lines for comments and service questions, pre-taped information, updates by phone and regular mailings with useful information and offers foster brand loyalty and opportunities for cross-selling of other products and services. Know also when *not* to utilize a pre-taped message. People calling service centers want to talk to real people.

Employee relations is a relatively young area of PR, likely a response to both litigation and political correctness. What was for a long time a seemingly incidental function of union reps or the personnel department, employee relations programs, well-executed, can reduce absenteeism, turnover, productivity and certainly lawsuits. Such programs, when publicized and exploited correctly, also go a long way to enhancing the public *image* of the employer.

Recognition awards; opportunities to participate in decisions; on-site child care; on-site continuing education programs; tuition reimbursement; sponsorship of employee special events and sports teams; company publications that both emphasize benefits, enhancement, accomplishments and recognize service and participation; health club memberships (or health club on-site); diet and wellness programs; jackets, rings, caps, shirts, pins and other elite team building devices: all promote employees' pride in being part of a well-respected organization that seems to respect them.

These devices all fit under the label of employee relations. Many of them are also employee *benefits,* but unlike health insurance, pensions and vacations, they promote an immediate perception that an employer respects contemporary concerns of employees that rise above payment for services rendered. In times of crisis, scandal or even minor difficulty, loyal employees are among the best spokespeople and representatives to the outside world an employer can have.

Event management, from an opening of a new facility to a celebration of an occasion, such as an anniversary, receipt or presentation of a major honor or award, to the ribbon-cutting of a new office or building: these are singular high-profile opportunities that may very well define how a person or an enterprise is perceived in the public's mind. Very often, the reference to the winner of a Clio, an Oscar, Emmy, Golden Eagle, Golden Trumpet, J.D. Powers Award, etc., becomes the *image marketing* designation that speaks volumes. It should have its own plan for publicity and promotion. Civic improvements or recognition such as a contribution to the enhancement of a public park or a school or the sponsorship of a literacy program or a scholarship or a fundraising event are only a few of the limitless ideas that can help identify you with something memorable and significant, apart from your ongoing program.

Governmental relations is the PR area most commonly referred to as *lobbying.* The lobbyist over the years has carried the image of the cigar-smoking sharp-talker with an envelope full of cash, ready to buy favors from government personnel through the "perfectly legal" purchases of vacation packages, ads in fundraiser programs or campaign contributions and business routed to businesses legislators own. Some of this has been true and sleazy. But mostly what lobbyists do is take their clients' cases to the government officials who might vote on regulation or legislation that could help or damage the lobbyist's clients or their industry.

Many lobbyists are lawyers and are extremely cautious in representing their clients or sharing their knowledge in the subjects they promote. Others, while not lawyers, are likely to be no less informed and certainly passionate in representing their case whether the issues are taxes, tariffs, children's television, gun control or tobacco. While pressure, persuasion and heightening public interest may be three methods of getting legislators' attention, frequently lobbyists are more effective away from "the glare of publicity." That doesn't mean what they're doing is wrong.

"Special interests" groups, as a term, has a decidedly unsavory tone. Yet, when the "special interests" being represented are the aged, the disabled, teachers or veterans, it doesn't sound so bad. And all of these groups have lobbyists carrying their story to various regulatory and legislative personnel at staff and executive levels. It is again the "spin control" applied to their efforts by persons of opposing points of view that try to make their presence seem somehow manipulative or dirty.

Lobbyists, of all PR professionals, have perhaps the most at stake. They are frequently representing the interests of entire industries, not just corporations. Yet they have done about the poorest job of presenting what they themselves do as honest and valuable.

Media and *press relations* is what most people mean when they use the term "PR." This is the publicist—the press agent—the practitioner who gets the client that important story in the important newspaper or magazine or that appearance on the important TV program.

It is true that some publicists are well-known and well-represented by certain powerful editors and producers. That, however, does not assure an interview, appearance or a story. The folks in key media jobs don't put their jobs at risk by giving prime space and time to particular stories just because the PR person is good or known to them. The key is newsworthiness.

What the competent PR specialist *can* do in some situations is find a unique, timely, unusual or fascinating way of presenting a person or story that might interest an editor or producer who might have otherwise taken a pass. Or present a source with a different point of view. But again, there must be something there to work with. Many media agencies or PR people will just "work the averages" which can be alright as well. That's when a story is fed to a large number of media outlets on the theory that *somebody* out there will carry it. It may not be the most prestigious media and it leaves the client inevitably asking "what comes next?"

Which, by the way, is an excellent question. The solution is to find uniqueness, interest and value in what you do and, by following your marketing plan, generate interest that builds, usually over your time line—not overnight. It is also a good idea to be realistic about the news value of what you have. Without question, major media exposure, at any time in your career or your company, product or service's existence can create a huge jump in interest and demand or it can do major damage. This again speaks to the need to *carefully* create and nurture public perceptions, rather than going for the high-risk strategy of hype and sensationalism—for which, incidentally, there is always a market.

By "servicing the media" with substantive information; knowing when to use news releases and press conferences; carefully taking note of who follows what markets and industries and what they have already done and not done, you are in a better position to effectively solicit and receive media attention and coverage.

Member relations can be a vastly complex area of public relations . . . or not. It depends on the size and nature of one's membership. For example, in some instances the term *member* is merely for status, substituting for the word "customer." Credit card companies, video and book clubs, warehouse stores all use the term *member* or refer to *member's price* or *member's rates*. Yet, since membership is pretty much open to anyone and the governing "rules" are vague, general and only binding in the most nominal sense, such members are actually "customers" and any program developed as a customer or client relations program could be applied here.

Memberships, however, such as a seat on the New York Stock Exchange, Chicago Board of Trade or National Association of Securities Dealers (NASD) are quite a different matter. Here, membership *truly* has its privileges. Membership allows a franchise to do business often under circumstances that are near or similar to a monopoly on certain types of transactions. Rules, regulations, protocols, and procedures fill volumes. News of changing laws or regulations or significant industry developments can mean life-or-death shifts in members' ways of doing business. A violation of a rule may not only carry a heavy fine or other sanction, but may constitute grounds for criminal prosecution.

Clearly, member relations in this context is a weighty responsibility in itself, providing timely and important information in the form of bulletins, alerts, memos and newsletters, as well as being both a repository for reference data and a resource. Trade association members may be located in far-flung reaches of the country or the world. Keeping attuned to the needs and desires of the members and reporting critical developments or just helpful tips is often a major undertaking. It is also an opportunity to advance the value and status of a membership by coordinating activities and developments, publicizing the positive and framing the negative, to whatever degree possible, in a context that diffuses hurtful impact.

Computer technology makes possible networks throughout which members can communicate instantaneously, but it also provides opportunities for misinformation. Rules of the road for the information superhighway will have to be enforced to maximize benefits of better communication and the member relations representative should be a qualified "traffic cop" to moderate, maintain and correct the flow and quality of information.

Publications are not always regarded as public relations vehicles. They are—or should be. Whether the publication is a quarterly newsletter, annual report, self-published newspaper or magazine, trade magazine or a brochure, it is an opportunity to present information that influences and informs. Those who believe an annual or interim report should be a "no-frills" financial document are missing a chance to enhance an image, reinforce investor and constituent confidence and commit to public record the perspective and personality of an enterprise. Financial sections speak for themselves, but annual and interim reports are often held on file or used as reference for journalists for years to come. A "president's (or chairman's) message" is an opportunity to create a context for good news, bad news, history or future plans that will serve as reference sources in the future.

Newsletters that were once mere "house organs" of company gossip and information have taken on a respectability and credibility previously unaccorded. Newsletters customized to present information to shareholders, the media, employees, regulators, customers, clients, prospects, retired employees and the financial community, represent a platform for carefully framed proposals, survey excerpts, editorials, and horn-blowing. A newsletter's abbreviated length and reader-friendly, nonintimidating format promotes readership, enhancing its likely influence vs. longer-length publications. Important newsletters and memos find their way out of the company. Know this and take advantage of it.

Fidelity Funds and Philip Morris are only two of the growing number of companies that have created their own regularly published magazines and they look great. The purpose is to use a format that appears friendly and familiar and present issues and opinions in the style of popular feature magazine articles. While entertaining and well-packaged, the motives are so obvious that even supporters of the companies tend to read such *sponsored* publications with a touch of skepticism. However well-done, a Philip Morris magazine appears blatantly intended to manipulate people's perceptions about smoking. To create such an impression runs counter to the aim of a long-term positive image. Attempting to manipulate public opinion is ambitious. Being accused of trying to do so can be devastating.

People believe the written word. Politicians or executives may claim they were misquoted in newspaper and magazine pieces and that their television or radio comments were taken out of context. Such clarifications, excuses and explanation frequently compound damage previously done. But a newsletter or direct mail brochure or catalog or a report that carries a "president's message," "editor's note" or "from the desk of . . ." carries weight. Someone has signed his or her name to a written statement, whether it is fact or opinion, and a signed column, letter or document—whether the reader agrees or disagrees with its conclusion—has some credibility. Using such documents effectively can be image enhancing. The public still seems to believe people who "put it in writing" are open and honest.

Research management as public relations involves using your research data for publicity purposes. Publishing the results of a market study or survey, at least its highlights and conclusion in an "executive summary," presents you as an industry observer as well as a participant and authority.

A questionnaire sent to clients or customers or prospects by itself provides you with useful data. The opportunity to return again to this audience with the results of the questionnaire—along with *your analysis*—of the results positions you in your industry or profession as a leader. A press release highlighting your comments on the results takes it another step, as does a by-lined feature article on the subject offered to a trade publication and a press release that your "definitive analysis" will appear there. The larger the survey or more in-depth the study, the greater the opportunity to merchandise it. A press release might be created, offering a copy of the results without charge to anyone who calls or writes to ask for it.

An alternative plan, of sorts, is to write an analysis of *someone else's* research—possibly even your competitors'—and follow the same dissemination procedures for your analysis as you would if you had written the material on which it is based yourself. Perhaps your experience or data contradicts published research—or supports it. It doesn't matter. What *does* matter is raising your own flag and creating the *perception* that you are as authoritative and knowledgeable as anyone else who would seek to gain public attention for the subject at issue. There is nothing inappropriate abut your exploiting someone else's material with analysis or comment as long as you properly identify and credit that someone else and do not reproduce their work as your own. Good journalists will routinely ask people other than the study's author to comment on its conclusions. By not waiting to be called, you are nonetheless advancing your image as a quotable authority on the subject.

Where the line is crossed between legitimate analysis and exploitation or opportunism is in both the content and the packaging of your material—the ongoing battle between style and substance. If your analysis has quality of content and is thoughtfully presented, it will have merit and value equal to the conclusion of the work on which you are commenting.

Shareholder relations / financial relations are two related, but separate functions. There is certain information a shareholder—

*Everything you want to know about
your competitors in one fell swoop.*

Introducing Peer Scape
The height of competitive insight.

Powerful and swift, Peer*Scape* from Deloitte & Touche LLP is a higher form of financial performance benchmarking.

Virtually overnight, Peer*Scape* brings you a comprehensive analytical and benchmarking package that provides a unique perspective on the competitive landscape.

Using crystal-clear charts and graphs, Peer*Scape* gives you a dramatic overview of your company's performance compared to its industry — or to any other peer group. Using not only SEC-mandated measures of shareholder return, but over 45 crucial comparative variables, including such measures as cost of capital, sales per employee and leverage.

Delivered to your door on one CD-ROM or in one convenient book, Peer*Scape* is fully customized: You can create the peer group you want to examine from

a list of 9,000 publicly traded companies and U.S. exchange-listed ADRs.

Updated annually or quarterly, Peer*Scape* may show you that your company is outperforming the competition in ways that Wall Street hasn't yet recognized. Reveal areas where there's room for improvement. Or identify unexpected strengths — and hidden weaknesses — in your competitors.

Best of all, with its broad perspective and powerful vision, Peer*Scape* could help you spot an important industry trend that's only beginning to appear on the horizon. The kind of trend your competitors — who still do performance benchmarking from ground level — won't see until it's directly overhead.

**Deloitte &
Touche LLP**

CALL 1-800-DELOITTE.

Deloitte Touche Tohmatsu International

EXHIBIT 2.3

Deloitte & Touche LLP

Deloitte & Touche offered a competitive performance research analysis on either CD–ROM or in book form to make a highly complex process accessible. That the software is marketed by a leading accounting and consulting firm underscores its image of thoroughness and reliability.

an owner of stock in an enterprise—must be provided by law. But the ongoing communication beyond what is required is what very often determines if a shareholder purchases additional shares, keeps those already owned when value declines or profit-taking is tempting, and if the stock is recommended to others. Such decisions are a function of the shareholders' perception of the enterprise, its management and its potential.

Would communications with shareholders be addressed through "media relations," such as a story appearing in the *Wall Street Journal*? The answer is *yes*, to a degree. The media will only devote a certain limited space to any story and will almost always present the material with its own interpretation and analysis. Any story that is worth giving to the media is worth giving to the shareholders in detail and with management's analysis, not a reporter's.

Further, people who have invested in a particular company or venture frequently resent having to learn the status of such ventures first in the media. Investors typically believe—very correctly—that they have a right to know where their money is going before disinterested other people know of it. The question then becomes one of trafficking in "insider information"—telling current shareholders something that should give them an unfair advantage over other investors in the stock market. Granted, there is a line to be walked here. Shareholders, though, are technically and legally the "owners" of a company, thus having their investments at risk with the company's fortunes at all times. They deserve to participate in an ongoing dialogue with management as to future plans under consideration, alternative courses for expansion, acquisition, merger, divestiture or new products or services and make informed decisions on that basis.

Certainly, it is not in the investors' interests that a company give away a "competitive edge" by saying too much too soon. Yet, neither is it in the company's interests to leave investors in the dark. As noted under *employee relations,* in bad times, the best friends a company can have are those with a vested interest in not only its survival, but its continuing to prosper. By keeping shareholders informed through newsletters, alerts, bulletins, videos, letters and a "shareholders' hotline" for information, you help maintain positive perceptions among investors in good times, bad times and even those flat periods when more attention-getting stocks seem more attractive. A shareholder acting with a knowledge that a company may do any number of things, is not acting on "insider information."

Financial relations, while largely relating to the same material content of information gathered and disseminated to shareholders speaks also to the financial or investment community of business writers and editors, securities analysts, banks, money managers and financial advisors, as well as portfolio managers and institutional investors. This group is largely regarded as the collective constituency that can make or break a public company. Charts, graphs, financial activity over a period of years and biographies of members of management are of concern to members of this group. No amount of statistical data is likely to be too much. Having offered that, it is important to know that major financial backers have extended seven-figure loans and lines of credit to a number of entrepreneurs over the years, based largely on their *image*. Under scrutiny, the numbers didn't add up. But when a *Time* or *Fortune* magazine cover calls you "hot" and suggests that investors are lined-up around the block trying to become involved with your next project, bankers, too, have been known to believe what they read, jump on the bandwagon and check the financial print-out later.

That is not to suggest that some of the most astute and sophisticated financial minds in the world are not easily duped. It is merely to suggest that, for all the sophistication and intelligence, they, too, can be dazzled and charmed. The best planned and best executed image marketing campaigns, however, still should be of substance, as depending on dazzle to carry the day is a pretty risky proposition under the best of circumstances.

Speechwriting is a function of public relations and, while it might seem like it should be an assumed part of the mix of agency services, it usually isn't and should be defined separately. Some people hate making speeches and try to ignore making them. Others are extroverted or merely pretty full of themselves and take the idea of writing and/or delivering a speech for granted. Both sides need to rethink their positions. What more dramatic impression might someone get from you than that based upon what you've been heard to say?

A speechwriter is rarely involved in most other PR functions. Like a survey or study, a good speech, with short, memorable quotes and a lot of substantive information, can be distributed— all or in part—by a publicist over time and generate interest long after the speech has ended. Excerpts can be featured in press releases, newsletters, backgrounders, and in published form as articles.

Where the speech is delivered can often be as important as the speech itself. If delivered at an industry function, a convention or to a regulatory group, it will imply significantly greater importance than to have been given to a smaller group at an executive's luncheon. Where one is invited to speak and the content of the speech itself—rich in quotes and repeatable soundbites—will very often serve to enhance the image of the speaker.

Many executives, public officials and others speak at any and all functions to which they are invited. While gracious, this is not necessarily the best way to enhance one's image. Have a reason to give a speech or an appearance. If media is covering your speech, a possibility at times even at a small trade group gathering, and your best remarks are reported, you have preempted their importance in other appearances. A small group may be delighted to hear an entertainer perform the same hits over and over, but no one wants to hear the same speech more than once. Be selective about what you say and where you say it. Insist that your speech and its presentation site be consistent with the image you wish to attain or maintain.

Speakers will sometimes ad lib their remarks, insisting their experience and position enables them to "wing it." Often this creates an impression of being ill-prepared, indifferent, disorganized or insecure. These are not regarded as especially positive traits, as perceptions go. Unfortunately, all speakers are not such great storytellers, nor need to be. Every speaking class will stress that it is bad form to read a speech, that speeches should be memorized and essentially performed. In the best of all situations, it does make a better presentation, but keep in mind that the emphasis should be placed on content over performance skills—substance over style. Reading a speech, referring to notes or an outline is far preferable to rambling on.

DELIVERING YOUR MESSAGE

Advertising and public relations in their various shapes and forms, largely constitute the Avenues of Awareness that can be utilized to take your presence and your message to a specific public or a variety of publics: to disseminate information in such a manner as to ensure *that* people become aware of you, your product, service or company, and to influence the way they perceive you. Every technique doesn't work every time for everyone. But the basic formula approach is solid.

The foundation of your effort is your marketing plan. It will guide you as to which avenues to pursue to generate awareness.

Exhibit 2.4 shows how interrelated the elements are:

- What is your situation, according to your own knowledge and what your research tells you?

- What is your objective? What is it you want to accomplish, according to your desires, goals and aspirations? What does your research tell you that you need to accomplish that may not be included in your own objectives statement?

- What strategy addresses your objective(s)?

- What tactics need to be employed to implement your strategy?

- How long will it take? Is this realistic?

- How much will it cost? Is this realistic to fund your strategy to meet your objectives within your timeframe?

In creating an image, you will find that some people will be receptive, open and attentive. Some will be impressed, some minds

EXHIBIT 2.4

Elements of a Marketing Plan

changed. Others will be unconvinced as to the merit of your case, no matter what you do. If you listen to the voice of the market and respond with a product, a service or a message of value, you will find an audience and some noticeable change.

In a 1991 collaboration published by the Harvard Business School Press, Vincent P. Barabba of General Motors and Professor Gerald Zaltman of the University of Pittsburgh wrote, "Even small improvements in learning about the marketplace and in the creative use of market information can have a major effect in eliciting more favorable responses to a firm's offerings."

"Eliciting more favorable responses" to one's offerings is certainly a good start.

On the subject of starts, a sign in a salesman's office read, "Nothing happens until somebody sells something." While that is an interesting premise, consider another idea—a variation, if you will—that might read, "Nothing happens until people are presented with choices of things offered to them for sale."

Before there can be a decision, there must be alternatives. A choice among alternatives will be made based on perceptions. Both statements offered have to do with creating actions, that is, with making everything happen.

Offer the information—the choices—and make something happen.

AT A GLANCE: THE TOOLS

1. To reach a level of public awareness where the impact of your image is felt takes time, financial backing and a plan.
2. Advertising and public relations provide marketers the processes to create, influence and maintain public perceptions.
3. Corporate advertising's objective is to make you or your company a better known *name.*
4. Image advertising's objective is to influence how people think of you.
5. Very occasionally, a corporate and an image message can be embodied into a single line or message that leaves a lasting, powerful impression.
6. Product advertising is to distinguish the characteristics of your product or service from those of the competition.
7. To fragment or cannibalize an ad budget to support a promotion, rather than to promote a product, company or image is a terrible dilution of resources.
8. The cornerstone of your effort to create and maintain awareness is your marketing plan.
9. The essential elements of an effective marketing plan are: a situation analysis, objectives, strategy and tactics, timeline and a realistic budget to accomplish the objective within the established timeframe.
10. Advocacy advertising is a bold decision that could be great or disastrous. It means going out on a limb and taking a potentially controversial or unpopular stand and perhaps winning new respect and support or offending and alienating some who may now support you. Be committed, sincere and choose carefully.

11. The first rule of effective public relations is not just to look good, but to *be* good. PR professionals can usually find something good to say about almost anything or anybody, but they cannot simply make bad look good.

12. Every technique won't work every time for everyone, but a solid foundation—your marketing plan—should get results if you use your research and clearly define your objectives, strategy and budget.

13. In creating and maintaining an image, know that some people will be receptive and open, some impressed, some minds changed and some will be totally resistant to anything you do. Expect it and be realistic.

14. Listening to the voice of the market will provide information to give a product with substance, a marketing plan of substance.

The Market Climate and the Halo Effect

It is said that "timing is everything" and certainly even the cynics among us are inclined to agree that, no matter how well you plan and how hard you try, to everything, there is a season. Luck, also, seems to play a role in success and failure. And prayer. And positive thinking. In all the volumes recounting success stories, these same words appear, often with phrases like "an idea whose time has come."

The fact is, though, timing is *not* everything. Throughout the history of business, there are countless tales of people, products and companies that should not have succeeded for any number of reasons, including that it was "the worst possible time" to undertake such a venture.

The Chicago Board Options Exchange was a new securities exchange launched by the Chicago Board of Trade in 1973. Prolonged market doldrums and trading volume at the lowest levels in years on the established exchanges made it a poor time to start a new exchange. Yet the Options Exchange not only succeeded; it became a major factor in rejuvenating established markets and inspiring a half-dozen imitators over the decade that followed.

So much for starting at the worst possible time.

A classic ad campaign recounted moments when, for a variety of products and reasons, "they said it couldn't be done . . ." yet success followed.

In *Getting It Right the Second Time,* Michael Gershman recounts stories of successful enterprises that became household names only after first being introduced and failing. Among them:

- Pepsi-Cola, which went bankrupt *three times* before becoming a leading soft drink around the world.

- Instant coffee, introduced in 1901, was a flop because people were not only used to drinking brewed coffee, but felt they had the time and inclination to make it.

- Jell-O, that classic gelatin dessert, could wobble all it pleased, but no one cared when it first appeared in 1897. It took a door-to-door product sampling campaign five years to generate interest.

The stories go on and on with claims of "the market just wasn't ready" as an excuse for failure or a touch of folklore for success. Sales managers have long held, however, that you make your own breaks and that those who wait for the most favorable market climate, when conditions are just right, will probably starve. There will never be a shortage of excuses or people to blame when something fails.

Notice the number of commercials that use the phrase "there was never a better time to buy" in spots that run all year-round, year after year. Then there is the year-end clearance sale, the end-of-season sale, the factory overstock sale, the introductory sale and enough other ways to say "just-get-in-here-and-buy-it-now" to fill this book. Good marketers have created their own "seasons" and reasons to buy.

Is there an ideal time or a worst possible time to launch a marketing campaign?

The salesperson's answer that you make your own breaks is the closest to being right, but the guiding rule should be common sense, a previously unmentioned component of your marketing plan. If *image marketing* is a factor—wanting to create a feeling or perception along with awareness—extra care should be taken.

For example, a United States senator had been contemplating announcing his candidacy for president for a very long time. This should have surprised no one. Most senators entertain such ideas. What *did* surprise many people was that he went ahead and made his announcement at a time he had obviously scheduled well in advance, having arranged the hall, the crowd, the banners and the usual trappings. The problem was that earlier that same day, a major terrorist bombing had killed more than a hundred people and had become the sole focus of the news media and the nation's attention as each hour brought fresh information updates.

The senator, a very skillful, bright and well-regarded person among citizens and fellow politicians, went ahead with his announcement on his schedule and found his story on page 11 of the papers and as a footnote on the TV newscasts. Worse yet, by focusing on his personal ambitions at a time when his colleagues and fellow countrymen were praying for survivors and mourning the tragic deaths of victims, his announcement seemed not merely ill-timed, but insensitive.

This specific example is used only because it is true and recent. Yet, the same principle applies if the subject is a new product announcement by a computer company, or a research lab with a health study or a new restaurant or theater or a superstar with a world concert tour schedule. The results would have been the same. Under such circumstances as a terrorist attack, an earthquake, a hurricane or tornado or a fire that leaves innocent people hurt, homeless or dead and communities shaken, marketing opportunities—particularly *image marketing* opportunities—still exist, but they must be handled with care, sensitivity and a sense of priority.

The senator could have put out a press release saying that he had reserved a hall, collected a crowd for a rally, and planned to announce his candidacy for president, but was instead, canceling the rally, postponing his official announcement and flying to the scene of the disaster to offer his support and whatever assistance he could provide the local officials and the community.

A political move? Opportunistic?

Sure.

But this approach would have allowed him to launch his campaign, however altered, while not being insensitive and not being swept aside by events and ignored. This approach also would have helped project an image of concern for the public good and the ability to establish priorities: a sense that he knew when and how to use his influence to do some good.

Of course, hopefully, each day's news headlines won't be dominated by terrorist bombings, earthquakes and hurricanes. But the time line of your marketing plan should include room to alter or modify the plan if extenuating circumstances require it.

The research that helps you to construct your marketing plan should tell you more than that people spend more time outdoors in the summer and buy more blankets in the winter. Your research should tell you the characteristics of the "market climate" in terms of what your constituent groups believe is important to them and to those they influence and those who influence them.

If fear of a possible recession or inflation is top of mind among your target audience, consider the timing, as well as the "packaging" of your message if increased or rising prices are a part of it. If environmental issues are dominating the news or public consciousness, show sensitivity to such concerns in your message or program.

Market research professionals do more than create a litany of likes and dislikes of a particular group or market segment. Their use of terms like "taking the pulse" and "listening to the voice" of the market reflects a reading of perceptions and emotions. Politicians don't win support by simply knowing what voters like and dislike, but by knowing their fears, anxieties, prejudices and dreams. Billions of dollars have poured into life insurance companies over the years because salespeople read people's fears and dreams and promised to be there with money for either or both.

Reflecting an awareness of such emotions and perceptions is hugely important to both the success of your effort and the image you create and project in pursuing it.

But having an understanding and sensitivity to a market climate does not mean letting it stop you from achieving your objectives. It means giving thought to finding ways of making that understanding work for you. Top salesmen don't wait for market conditions to get better. Top salesmen are out there *selling* without excuses why they can't and regardless of market conditions.

Some politicians believed it was important to be the first to declare his or her candidacy for a particular race or to declare sometimes fully a couple of *years* before an election. The claim is that the candidate needed extra time to become better known and to get his message across.

Nonsense.

That sort of approach may have been necessary when campaigning was done on horseback, but since 1960, we know that one television "debate" has the potential to put all candidates—the first and last to declare—on an even level. If the personality and the message, the *presence*—the *image*—is a winner, the candidate is likely to be a winner, even if he or she was an unknown before the "debate." Debates notwithstanding, John F. Kennedy in 1960, Eugene McCarthy in 1968, George Wallace also in 1968 and Ross Perot in 1992 have all shown over time that a single incident, appearance, speech or "moment" can catapult a candidate from the lesser ranks to major contender status.

A MOMENT IN TIME

And the process is not limited to politics. Each year a significant number of unknown people and companies take advantage of an incident—a moment—to exploit circumstances to build public image, businesses and careers.

Ralph Nader was an unknown attorney in the 1960s when his book *Unsafe at Any Speed* was published and his appearance on national television to promote the book, virtually overnight, won him the designation of America's number one consumer advocate. Volunteers, mostly college students, lined up to help him take on the giants of the auto industry and other corporate heavyweights. Without thought to market climate or timing, the Consumer Rights Movement was born and became something of an industry itself.

Another example of left field flukes, images and making the most of the moment involved Nancy Kerrigan and Tonya Harding, two figure skaters among many competing for places on the U.S. Olympic team. An attack on Ms. Kerrigan by persons close to Ms. Harding created a headline story that held public interest and dominated water cooler conversations for weeks. Images emerged of Ms. Kerrigan as the storybook princess, of sorts, attacked and nearly crippled, struggling to come back to the cheers of the crowd. Ms. Harding, on the other hand, was portrayed as a "bad girl" with a troubled past that included a shady husband and photos published in a national magazine to her detriment. For nearly a year, the story was a cottage industry with books, magazines and TV movies. On the strength of the images that emerged from literally a single day's worth of news coverage, with excellent "handling" by Ms. Kerrigan's representatives and clumsy reactions from Ms. Harding's people, Nancy Kerrigan signed seven-figure contracts that included endorsements, commercials, TV specials and appearances at Disney World. Tonya Harding appeared washed up as a figure skater and subsequently attempted to exploit her notoriety in B-movies and professional wrestling. Would Nancy Kerrigan's endorsements have been so lucrative had there not been a "moment" to exploit? We'll never know. But her managers knew how to turn a tragedy into an opportunity.

Elizabeth Ray, Donna Rice, Jessica Hahn and Brian "Kato" Kaelin are all people who confused an incident or a moment in the limelight with having a celebrity status, a public image and something to sell. Quick book deals, film cameos or TV interviews do not a career make, if the true substance—the product—is not there. To succeed, one cannot simply be "on the news." There must be a product or talent worth testing.

Such exploitation is not marketing, it is cashing in. And what these nice people believed to be their celebrity status proved to be not even a valid public image, but a footnote in pop culture.

If the product or service or entity to be marketed has substance, virtually *any* market climate (absent tragedies that overshadow everything else) is the right market climate.

That may seem a bit simplistic in view of the proliferation of "trend shops" foretelling the great changes that lie ahead and representing their predictions as science. Certainly, if a concern for emerging trends keeps you from committing to a plan, then "megatrends" likely keep you awake at night. Megatrends, as described in the book of that name by the publisher and consultant

John Naisbitt, addressed "Ten New Directions Transforming Our Lives." Its sequel offered "Ten New Directions for the 1990s."

With all due respect to Mr. Naisbitt and other futurists, to draw attention away from the simple basic elements of the marketing plan to address such "new directions" as "the Age of Biology" and "The Religious Revival of the New Millennium" sort of misses the point. As Nike put it so appropriately: *Just do it!*

Changes in the marketplace, shifts in power, will not cause your plan to be harmed or affected significantly if the basic plan is sound. The situation analysis, objectives, strategy, tactics take in the market climate of today, as well as potential shifts ahead. Quality survives and the *image* of quality illuminate it.

And illumination is somewhat the essence of "the halo effect." This, in a manner of speaking, is when success begets success, when the attraction and desirability of an entity is so strong as to benefit even peripheral people and things, related or unrelated.

For example, Michael Jordan is such a charismatic figure that his presence not only raises attendance figures at Chicago Bulls basketball games, but sells merchandise and creates demand for appearances and endorsements by his fellow teammates, as well as himself.

The fashion industry is a billion-dollar example of a halo being used to sell a product, where identification is as, or more, important than the product itself. James Brady wrote in *Superchic— Reporting Fashion,*

> Despite the high prices charged by the couture (an individual dress these days may cost closer to two thousand dollars than one thousand dollars), it is rare for a couturier to make any money on fashions. . . . Most great couture houses become rich through the sale of their private-label perfume. In fact, for many Paris houses, the couture collection is simply an event to attract publicity, to promote the name, so more of its own label perfume will be sold.

These words were written in 1974 and more than 20 years later are still a textbook example of using a halo as a brand. What Chanel, Dior, Pierre Cardin and Yves St. Laurent learned to be the case with Paris designs in the seventies is a reality of life for Ralph Lauren, Calvin Klein, and American designers today. It

EXHIBIT 3.1

Swiss Army Brand

The Swiss Army Knife has an image of versatility, reliability and no-nonsense functionality. To transfer such an image to the highly competitive category of wristwatches, the Swiss Army brand skipped the subtlety and delivered the message in an appropriately no-nonsense way.

would be unthinkable to expect to successfully introduce a line of clothing without one eye to what related or even unrelated businesses and industries might be developed.

Windham Hill Records became identified not only with the work of George Winston and guitarist Will Ackerman, but very strongly with the type of "new age" jazz they performed. Therefore, music lovers would buy albums of original material by unknown performers based on their belief in an image of what the label and its artists—any artists—would deliver.

The halo effect can provide a type of brand extension status though sometimes without the brand. It is the acceptance of an image of something based on its relationship to something else. In many respects, it is image marketing at its most effective. When a constituent or constituent group feels good about something, it is not unusual for that good feeling to be transferred to something else seen as related to it.

A short-cut to image marketing is to make use of the halo effect—to identify with an entity that has an image to which you aspire. The key is to identify with that entity while creating or maintaining a separate identity. For example, some products or companies will run comparison ads on TV or radio commercials, singling out a value feature of their product, while positioning it directly against a brand that is far better known. The direct or implied message is that the lesser known product has everything the category leader has and more.

Products of every sort seek to benefit from the halo effect by including the line "from the makers of . . ." or "from the producers of . . ." in ads, press releases and other materials, suggesting that the market's acceptance of one product, service or entity, should imply a willingness to accept a presumption of goodwill for something else from the same "family."

Salesmen are fond of saying that their best prospects are their current customers, having already been sold at least once. Attempts at cross-selling occur, assuming the customer's satisfaction with one product will lead to the customer being at least receptive to try another from the same "maker."

Sears, Roebuck & Company, for generations the "World's Largest Store," tried carrying its department store approach to the

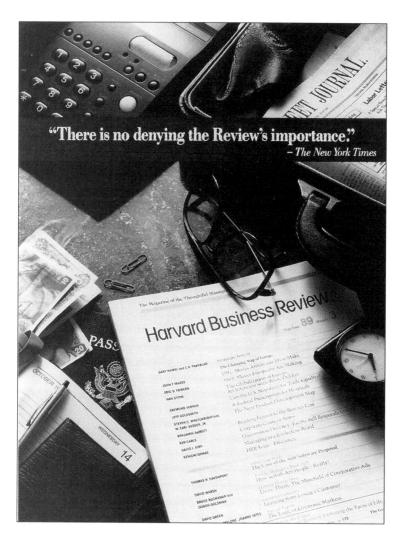

EXHIBIT 3.2

Harvard Business Review
A fine magazine for the crowded business publication market uses as its slogan "The Magazine of the Thoughtful Manager." Yet, despite its excellence, without question its circulation derives to its greatest extent from its parentage, the Graduate School of Business Administration of Harvard University. The singular status and image of the University carries the power to sell the magazine. No matter how high the level of quality, if it were called the "State University Business Review" no one would care.

financial services industry. Apparently, Sears management assumed that if customers believed the store had quality retail goods, they would feel the same about real estate and mutual funds. So Sears acquired the real estate firm of Coldwell Banker and the securities brokerage of Dean Witter Reynolds. Fitting its long-held Allstate Insurance into the mix, the company formed the Sears Financial Network.

While management assumed the Sears name would carry a certain degree of clout in the market, they were disappointed. Investors felt good enough about the professionalism of Dean Witter that the Sears name really added little. Ditto Coldwell Banker. In this case, there was light, but no halo. The Sears name didn't hurt, but it also didn't help. Wall Street viewed this miscalculation as a negative regarding Sears' management's judgment.

Sears perhaps cannot be faulted for seeking further diversification, but attitude and awareness research likely would have suggested that, to become successful as a new entity, the Sears Financial Network would have to do more than put the Sears name on a series of separately existing entities. They would have had to create a new perception of value or value-added to the existing companies. In this case, the Sears "halo" was not bright enough to automatically benefit anything it chose to cover without showing that added value.

The halo effect as a marketing device is not the same as launching a brand extension or licensing the use of your name for an unrelated product, although obviously there are some similarities in the process' objectives—to help use the power of one entity to sell something else. As noted, sometimes an entity can benefit from its identification with something else, even if that something else is a competitor—or perhaps an important name in a foreign market. In that regard, the halo effect also is not necessarily an endorsement by the entity from which it seeks to receive benefit.

The advertising strategy that uses "borrowed interest" is like the halo effect in that it offers a suggestion of a clear connection between entities, (although each clearly retains its independent identity). The idea of borrowed interest, however, does have one foot in the endorsement camp, reflected in the use of product placements. They might be paid for outright or featured in exchange for their use, such as when a hotel is used as an important location in a TV show or movie scene. Similarly, when someone in a film flies United Airlines, orders "a Coke," uses a Polaroid camera, lights up a Marlboro, or drives off in a BMW, there is a subtle or implied product endorsement. More specifically, the products are often used to define a character's image by identifying with a product's image. And the reverse is also true: the product is, to some extent, identified with the image or quality of its use in the placement.

BADGES, BANNERS, LOGOS AND FLAGS

In creating an image as identified in your marketing plan, such elements as borrowed interest and the halo effect are helpful and expedient. So, too, is the state of the *brand* as it evolved in modern times. To project an image of success or status, one no longer needs an entourage, trumpets and a limo driver.

If the image to which you aspire can benefit from the halo effect, review those elements already associated with that image in the minds of your constituents and develop a strategy and tactics to identify you with them. Your research should be able to guide you in this area. Are your constituents:

- Older?
- Younger?
- Both?
- Baby boomers?
- Men?
- Women?
- Both?
- Parents of very young children?
- Children with elderly parents?
- Sports fans?
- Music lovers?
- Patriotic?
- Responsive to funny ads?
- Readers?
- Investors?
- Avid coupon clippers?
- Religious?
- Retired?
- Students?
- Ethnic minorities?
- Affluent?
- Conservative?

You can march to your own drummer, be all that you can be, have it your way and pretty much every other thing that allows you to ignore the voice of the market if you want to fail. But, while exploiting your value and uniqueness, give some consideration to the rules that have served some of the most successful retailers in American business history:

- Put the customer first
- Give the customer what he wants
- The customer is always right

Can you retain your individualism and the uniqueness of what you have to offer without upsetting your constituents comfort level?

Robert L. Dilenschneider, CEO of The Dilenschneider Group, offers this advice: "Understand how people see things, then appeal to what they prefer. The key to real image strategy is understanding the link between how people see and what people prefer."

It is important also to watch what people do, more than what they say. While it would be speculative and certainly impolite to suggest that people lie to researchers, there certainly is a segment that responds with what they think is the "right answer," what they think people want to hear, and what they think is the answer that makes them look bright. Pay attention to what people actually buy and do. Note that people are often reluctant to admit being a part of a great social mass that indeed makes up that common denominator.

People's buying decisions are based largely on *value* and *image.*

Value is the combination of price and quality—the right price for an acceptable or better level of quality.

Image is the more difficult factor to define and qualify because it is the reflection of very specific, yet individual emotions and perceptions. People do look at the same thing and see it differently. Creating an image to which they can respond somewhat predictably is the marketer's challenge. Without definitive research to support this position, consider the image of the hotter of the "hot buttons" that motivate people to buy. Image is, when projected correctly, that "feel good" quality.

BUZZWORDS

The following terms convey an "instant image." It may not be exactly the same image to everyone—height, weight, hair, color, sex, age and mileage may vary. One person's mental picture of a yuppie, for example, may be quite different than another's, but the imagery of what the term has come to represent should be common.

The uniqueness of a list such as this is that these are *image words* that should trigger both a picture and an emotion—affection, distaste, resentment, cynicism and personal recognition or identification.

Challenge yourself to see what pictures come to mind as you review the words and terms in Exhibit 3.3.

LIFESTYLE MARKETING

The 1980s proved to be a period of significant market polarization.

Lifestyle and niche campaigns can yield the narrowest markets and returns, and more importantly, alienate segments along the way. This is not to suggest that, when choosing media, women's pages and magazines, gay publications or ethnic publications can't be utilized for advertising and PR if their demographic reach is part of your plan's objective. But too often, special-focus marketing is transparent and the audience feels patronized or victimized. Concentrate on content as the safeguard in such cases. Attempting to ride a yuppie, "New Age" or some other trend that addresses lifestyle is not image marketing, it's gimmick marketing.

THE MESSAGE

Direct response ads on TV tend to pull well when the message includes a phrase such as "this exclusive offer," even though the offer is being made to anyone and everyone in range of the commercial. Still, the word "exclusive" conveys a sense of something special, important or privileged.

achiever	independent
award-winning	in-your-face
Baby Boomer	irreverent
beautiful people	jet-setter
bureaucrat	left wing
celebrated	liberal
conservative	liberated
correct	light
creative	limited
cutting edge	the media
distinguished	membership
ditsy	nerd
elitist	new age
exclusive	new breed
family values	premium quality
free	the press
free-spirited	right wing
fundamentalist	seniors
futurist	singles
Generation X	socially conscious
gifted	sophisticated
hacker	technology
hands-on	technocrat
hard-hitting	veteran
healthy	Woodstock
hippie	workaholic
hot	yuppie
humanitarian	

EXHIBIT 3.3

Image Words

The Madison Hotel in Washington, D.C., long identified itself on its letterhead, matchbooks, brochures and its advertising as "Washington's correct address." This gentle snob appeal spoke of a dignity, higher class and separateness typically identified with a bygone era, one many people consider preferable to the present for its emphasis on manners, prosperity and "correctness."

The new product was described as on the "cutting edge." The phrase offers nothing by way of descriptions and is all imagery. Yet, it carries a sense of strength and innovation.

Few terms are more personally subjective than "creative," yet it carries a big promise and is applied—and misapplied—to a wide variety of practices and products. Serious marketers should look for "viability" as an underpinning of creativity and not allow the term to be used as a carte blanche excuse or explanation for any manner of things. Too often, applying the term artistic or creative to something is supposed to give it a validation in itself.

Forget it.

Marketing plans and programs need to be grounded in reason. Companies, products, careers and dollars depend on it. Getting an award for creativity is a small consolation if awareness and acceptance of our marketable entity fails to materialize.

What can the halo effect directly or indirectly offer marketers?

To start, credibility and authority.

Advertising professionals who try to make a case for advertising on an intellectual level, contend that one reason even marginal advertising can be persuasive and effective is that, despite the denials and protestations, viewers of advertising are willing to suspend their belief and convey an assumption of credibility and authority to an ad's message. The sense of it is that the media would not even allow an ad to appear if it contained fraudulent claims or untruths. This is the same mind-set that has people willing to believe that something is true if it is printed in a newspaper or reported on a news broadcast. Most of us deny our acceptance of this premise, yet we then do go on to repeat what we've heard as fact.

On one level, it would seem this suggestion insults the intelligence of the public. The simple fact is, news reporting is largely superficial due to time and space limitations and a "quick fix" of news and information has been the choice of the public for years. As to the reliability of the information, it is true that, whether news or paid advertising, all media follow defined standards and practice guidelines for accuracy and truthfulness and no respectable media knowingly misrepresents.

But liberties are indeed taken, exaggeration is permitted, and rarely is heard a discouraging word.

During the Watergate hearings, the Congressional response to a political scandal and constitutional issues, Senator Sam Ervin, 76 years old, overweight, rumpled and possessing a very pronounced North Carolina drawl, liked to describe himself as "just a little ol' country lawyer." Reporters would laugh and then report that Mr. Ervin was one of the senate's great constitutional scholars. That description of him was picked up and repeated without challenge over and over again. It was universally accepted as fact.

This is not to suggest that Senator Ervin was *not* a Constitutional scholar or, for that matter, that he was not a little ol' country lawyer. It is only to note that the general public never requires proof of such characterizations or questions references to credentials.

How does the public know that someone is really a "respected expert" on Middle Eastern affairs, underwater exploration, laser technology, nutrition and the stock market?

We know because they were introduced or described thusly by a polite and seemingly informed reporter or news anchor . . . who quite likely received such information from the expert's public relations representative or a press kit, noting the number of speeches the expert has delivered on the subject. Unless the expert is making claims or observations so outrageous and inflammatory as to set red lights flashing, resumes are simply accepted, introductions made and credibility accorded. This has become an accepted practice over time because most people are who they say they are and are representing something that pretty much does what they say it does.

Designations like well-respected, expert, authority, and even brilliant or genius are handed out liberally with coffee during an interview because such descriptions and references make for a more interesting story.

The process has evolved to be this:

The public knows that someone or something is worthy of our attention because the media, or in the case of speakers, our host organization, has told us so and we believe them.

The public knows that a particular person or product is "hot" or is "sweeping the country" or "catching on" or "turning heads" or "flying off the shelves" or "the rage of South America" because it quite simply has been described virtually as such in the media.

The media received such a description and information from a public relations person who is believed by the media because of having carefully built up his or her reputation for integrity, accuracy and credibility. Usually.

Images are able to be created because people influence the opinions of other people, working from a carefully crafted marketing plan and following a process step by step.

AT A GLANCE: THE MARKET CLIMATE AND THE HALO EFFECT

1. There is no such thing as a "worst possible time" to launch a marketing campaign.
2. Common sense and market research should be the guide to the best market climate.
3. Be sensitive to environmental and emotional issues at a given period and how such factors might effect your plan.
4. The timeline of a marketing plan should allow for flexibility to modify or alter the plan if extenuating circumstances require it.
5. Be prepared to take advantage of an incident to create a marketing opportunity.
6. If a product, service or entity has substance, virtually any market climate is the right market climate.
7. Quality survives and the *image* of quality illuminates it.

8. The halo effect is when the attraction and desirability of an entity is so strong as to benefit even peripheral people and things, related and unrelated.

9. The halo effect supports the acceptance of an image of something, based on its relationship to something else.

10. The halo effect can provide a short-cut to image marketing by identifying with an entity while maintaining a separate identity.

11. Current customers are the best prospects for cross-selling opportunities for other products and services promoted in the reflected image of the purchased item.

12. Borrowed interest suggests a definite image relationship or implied kinship between entities.

13. If the image to which you aspire can benefit from the halo effect, review the elements that are associated with the image in the minds of your constituents and develop a strategy and tactics that will identify you with them.

14. While exploiting your individual value and uniqueness, emphasize putting the customers' interests first.

15. People's buying decisions are based on value and image.

16. Value is the combination of price and quality.

17. Image is the "feel good" quality that triggers emotions.

18. Creative is a subjective term that carries a big promise. Viability should be the underpinning of a creative program.

19. The public willingly suspends its belief system when it watches commercials and is receptive to suggestions of credibility and authority.

20. The public forms its own perceptions and opinions based on what the media presents.

21. Images can be created because people influence the opinions of other people, sharing not so much facts as their perceptions.

CHAPTER 4

The Ups and Downs of Endorsements and Sponsorships

Just as the halo effect hopes that the light of success from one entity might be exploited to benefit another and borrowed interest attempts to create a favorable identification between similar (or even dissimilar) entities, the use of a paid celebrity endorser of a marketable commodity provides yet another way to generate greater awareness and visibility without the person, product, company or service having to do a lot more than just exist.

If the image you want is already personified by a particular person with a high profile, the idea of publicly associating becomes too simple and obvious not to try. Simple and obvious, perhaps, but not without its potentially damaging side-effects.

Using paid celebrities in ads and for endorsements is, of course, not new. For years, a male sports figure hadn't really "made it" until he was signed to endorse Gillette razor blades or, the ultimate, to appear on boxes of Wheaties—*the breakfast of champions!* Both were extra money for the athlete, and his presence helped sales and helped to position and differentiate the products. A celebrity cutting the ribbon at the opening of a new supermarket or at the "christening" of a ship always was a sure

bet to attract a photographer or two from a paper or trade publication. A baseball bat or a catcher's mitt with a great athlete's
name on it could carry a higher price and still outsell those with
the names of merely a lowly manufacturer, even if the products
were exactly alike. A pro's name on golf balls and clubs has always
gotten the same reaction from the older kids. It was the power of
a big name to bring people into theaters—except, of course, this
time you got only the name and not the star.

But, no matter. Names associated with merchandise—famous,
good names, whether Babe Ruth on a bat or Arnold Palmer on a
golf ball—have traditionally meant sales.

The process of the celebrity endorsement has become a phenomenon. Despite the fact that Babe Ruth's name on a bat and
ball and his likeness in an ad can still sell products some three-
quarters of a century after his record year of 1927, the Babe, in
his day, never saw the kinds of fees or representation that an
athlete today would command for just a single TV commercial. And
the process has matured to where particular agents and agencies
are operating strictly as "celebrity brokers" and do nothing but
negotiate with and for celebrities not only in the sports and
entertainment fields, but in every profession and every industry.
For example, business magazines run ads that carry endorsements
from former astronauts and retired legislators. Quasi-public figures, from judges in high-profile cases to authors such as Kurt
Vonnegut, Norman Mailer and Gore Vidal, are sought to endorse
liquors, computers, fountain pens and virtually any product for
which an image might be deemed transferable. Former Fidelity
Mutual Fund guru, Peter Lynch, has become spokesman/endorser
for a business magazine, and real estate developer, Donald Trump,
has appeared in TV commercials for soft drinks and other products.

Three factors have emerged as critical in the celebrity endorsement field—and they are vastly more at issue than in the
days of Babe Ruth. They are:

1. cost

2. credibility

3. the crisis factor

Any one of these factors could represent minor problems or major disasters for a product, person, company or service and, quite possibly, for the entire industry in question.

COST

What's a name worth?

Once a company could get an endorsement from an entertainer or an athlete in exchange for a new car. Alas, that has not been the case for major celebrities for a long time. Depending on whose name is involved, the celebrity's price may be a considerable financial interest in the product or company itself. Basketball superstar Michael Jordan has received considerably more in fees from Nike, McDonald's and Chevrolet than he ever earned playing basketball.

In several instances, the announcement of a celebrity being signed to an endorsement contract became a major news item itself, such as Nancy Kerrigan signing with Disney or a former vice president of the United States agreeing to do a potato chip commercial. But no celebrity endorsement deal can yet match that of Pepsi and pop music star Michael Jackson, who signed for a reported $10 million. The impressive amount, perhaps the most lucrative in its time, was only a part of the story. The deal called for Mr. Jackson to appear in three television commercials, did not require that he use, mention, or even be seen in the same frame as the product or its name. The sense of anticipation accorded the first viewing of the first commercial was heightened by news billboards, promos and the kind of hype normally reserved for the Super Bowl rather than for the airing of a 30-second television commercial.

The image marketing was very effective. A superstar performer was identified with a product—whether he used it or not was irrelevant—his image matching its image of youth and energy with the association of excitement. Across the United States, across economic and generational lines, for weeks people everywhere were talking about Michael Jackson's Pepsi TV spot. Did it sell the product? That was not really the objective of the ads. These particular spots were to get people—particularly younger people, the product's prime demographic group—thinking about Pepsi and talking about Pepsi. The sales, it was believed, would logically follow in relative time proximity to the "top of the mind" awareness.

The advertiser professed to be delighted. Pepsi was one advertiser who could afford to be delighted. Not a lot of companies put $10 million into three TV spots, much less for a single talent fee.

This is a unique and exaggerated example, of course, but the number one question that is asked regarding celebrity endorsements is "Are they worth the money?" The resounding answer is *sometimes.* Consider:

- When the endorser and the endorsement do not upstage the product, person or company being endorsed, producing a comment like "You know—that Michael Jordan commercial with the car in it. . . ."

- When the research indicates that the celebrity's participation and identification are likely to help achieve the objective—increased sales, greater levels of awareness, market share, shelf space, customer loyalty to establish or change a market position or perception.

- When the cost of the celebrity's participation as a percentage of the budget will not result in reductions of quality elsewhere, such as in production value or media scheduling.

Then the use of a celebrity endorser could be just the right element to help advance your image.

Clearly, ads that feature a recognizable person get early and greater initial recognition. So the use of a celebrity, hitching a ride on another's star, may not be a bad idea. What must be determined from a strictly business perspective, however, is whether or not it is the *best* idea.

Fortunately, few celebrities are in the seven-figure range, yet cost should be no less a consideration. The greatest advantage a celebrity can bring to the process—the whole *point* of celebrity

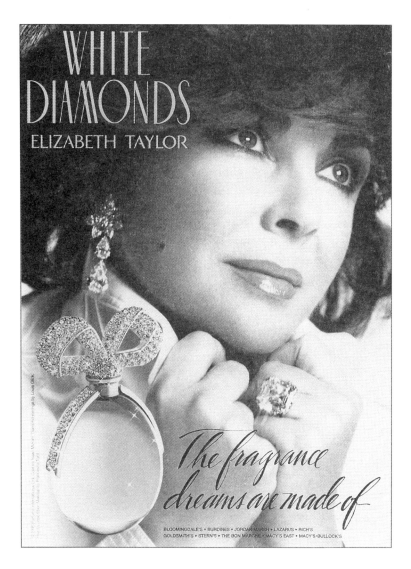

EXHIBIT 4.1

Parfums International
Elizabeth Taylor attained the status of being not only a legendary screen
personality and actress, but for years was described without qualification in the
media as "The Most Beautiful Woman in the World." The only thing perhaps as
compelling as her name on this fragrance is its total ad copy message: The
fragrance dreams are made of.

endorsements, actually—is that he or she must not only fit your image or the image to which you aspire, but the celebrity must already have a distinctive, recognizable image and be in a position to deliver his or her fans or admirers, suggesting to them through identification with you that you have a clear commonality with them. In such cases, the celebrity's ability to influence—to *deliver*—as opposed to just being recognized, becomes a major factor. Many familiar current and past familiar faces can be *recognized,* but is that enough? If they can't deliver a level of influence, might you do better with an attractive (or just as memorable) unknown model or actor who will cost a lot less? A checklist of the positive attributes of a celebrity being considered as an endorser should be evaluated against a non-celebrity to reassure you in your decision process.

A simple checklist will help you focus on the attributes and potential liabilities of a celebrity endorser vs. a non-celebrity. Some answers will be numbers or percentages, some "yes or no," others perhaps a number. The point is to have a single overview of whether or not the celebrity endorser is a good idea.

CREDIBILITY

Celebrities not only have their fans and admirers, but their detractors, a situation that is less of a concern with the less well-known model or actor. Even huge stars and other high-profile personalities have been known to evoke the response, "Boy, I really hate that guy." One of our objectives is creating and defining the image to minimize the negative. A celebrity who comes with "baggage" may get recognized, but is that all you want?

Please remember in such cases not to let "relative" research get in the way. Because the CEO and his or her family like a particular celebrity is not reason enough to get out your checkbook.

Advancing image by identifying with a celebrity can be a shrewd move, unless the fit of your image and that of the celebrity seems like a mismatch to your audience.

Bill Cosby was as strong a celebrity presenter as ever performed the task for Jell-O. But for the investment firm of E. F.

	Celebrity	Non-Celebrity
1. Cost as a % of budget		
2. Has currently or recently endorsed another entity		
3. Is strongly identified with another product or company		
4. Has appeared in (number) of commercials and ads over his or her career		
5. Is identified with a trend or fashion style		
6. Is regarded as controversial		
7. Is likely to alienate certain market segments		
8. Has a track record of attracting attention or delivering an audience		
9. Has potential for becoming involved in an issue or cause that could reflect negatively		
10. Has a complementing image		

EXHIBIT 4.2

Checklist: Celebrity—Non-Celebrity Endorsers

Hutton, the fine comic actor's serious, concerned counsel on choosing a broker just didn't ring true. The ads proved a major disappointment in their blatant failure to shore up the firm's image, which was then at a low point.

George C. Scott, long regarded as one of America's finest dramatic actors, was a very believable General Patton on screen, but a not-so-believable pitchman for Renault, the automobile badly in need of an image lift. John Wayne, in rugged western attire, on horseback, speaking straight into the camera lens about his headache and why he chose Datril pain reliever, proved to be, at its best moment, simply embarrassing.

In each of these cases, not only was the endorser better known than the product (not always a bad thing), but the images of the celebrity and the product together just did not ring true. As much as the public admired and respected these talented men, in these instances, they didn't believe them.

Credibility is also a consideration when a celebrity is overexposed as an endorser. The public has long known and accepted that celebrities are paid to endorse products and certain individuals, such as Dick Clark and Ed McMahon, became far better-known for their various commercials than for their other professional experiences. But when Mr. Cosby or Michael Jordan endorses so many products that they appear more to be simply cashing-in on their celebrity status, rather than sincerely recommending something they truly believe to be of value, they, the entities they represent and the public all lose. Football great Joe Namath endorsed so many products from popcorn makers to pantyhose to arthritis pain reliever, that he remained a recognizable presence in the ads, but had virtually no credibility as an influence.

Does the public believe that a baseball player who appears in an ad or an endorsement really uses a particular deodorant, mouthwash or after-shave lotion? Or that Jack Nicklaus knows anything at all about cellular phones? Or Paul Reiser knows the first thing about which is the best personal computer on the market?

Probably not. The purpose of the celebrity's presence is to get attention and if that's your only intention—to utilize the celebrity as a device to catch the eye of the audience—then anyone you can afford will do, from one of the Gabor Sisters to Arnold, the pig from the television show *Green Acres*.

EXHIBIT 4.3

Swatch

The Olympic Games are perhaps the most sponsored single event and Olympic medal winners are among the most sought after endorsers. In this ad for Swatch watches, the point is made that without time and time trials, there would be no Olympic games. Dan Jansen's presence takes the concept to a more personal level.

But if your objective is to create both visibility and credibility with your audience, while at the same time identifying your image with that of a celebrity who already *has* the image you want, then select a person who has a clear compatibility with the marketable entity *and* has credibility.

A list of celebrity spokespersons and endorsers could surely fill a book by itself. Sometimes the fit is right, sometimes not. In no particular order, Exhibit 4.4 shows some of the most memorable matchups—situations where the image of the celebrity seemed in perfect sync with the product.

Celebrity	Advertiser
Candice Bergen	Sprint
Bill Cosby	Jell-O, Kodak
Catherine Deneuve	Chanel
Joe DiMaggio	Mr. Coffee
Annette Funicello	Skippy peanut butter
James Garner & Mariette Hartley	Polaroid
Michael Jordan	Nike, McDonald's
Ricardo Montalban	Chrysler
Cybill Shepherd	L'Oreal
Brooke Shields	Calvin Klein
O.J. Simpson	Hertz
and the worst . . .	
Frankie Avalon	Zero-pain
Bill Cosby	E. F. Hutton
Madonna	Pepsi
Joe Montana	Franklin Mutual Funds
Dorothy Provine	Pristine
John Wayne	Datril

EXHIBIT 4.4

Memorable Celebrity/Product Matchups

CRISIS FACTOR

Perhaps the least considered factor in the decision to seek and use a paid celebrity endorser is the possibility that one day the celebrity will embarrass you or, worse yet, propel your association and identification with him or her into a mass of negative publicity or even a major scandal.

In the days of the so-called "Golden Age of Hollywood," the studio system prevailed. Actors, regardless of their age or popularity, were on the payroll of the major studios and under this arrangement, the studios essentially managed actors' lives. Marriages could be hastily arranged or undone to coincide with the release of the actor's next film. The huge studio publicity machine controlled entirely what the public knew or didn't know about someone, whether it was true or wholly manufactured to create or perpetuate "an image." Stories were planted and others "killed" on a regular basis.

That doesn't happen anymore. While there are still powerful agents and agencies with considerable influence in the media, the type of control they exerted as recently as the 1970s is gone. Veteran publicist Henry Rogers wrote in one of his volumes of memoirs "The relationship between the public relations man, the media and the client is always a delicate one and requires walking a tightrope every moment of the working day."

In an era of "ambush interviews" and "tabloid journalism," bad news is big news and even the most influential of network, studio or government people find themselves powerless to "kill" a scandalous or deeply personally revealing story. Such stories provide the best lessons of how an image might be set-back or destroyed completely.

Pepsi had the unique run of bad luck to have, within a short period of time, endorsement deals with entertainers Michael Jackson and Madonna and boxing champ Mike Tyson. All three celebrities were at the top of their game and having them was regarded as something of a coup for Pepsi. Until, that is, all three found themselves (individually) in situations ranging from embarrassing to scandalous. Pepsi, while pulling their ads featuring these three individuals, had to deal with the embarrassing questions about the private lives of high-profile people over whom they had no control.

The company talked about its support for the celebrities, clearly found some value in getting a lot of free publicity, but had to worry at each step that publicity of this type may have a short-term impact on sales and a long-term impact on a carefully cultivated image. Being the spokesperson or endorser for a product that says it's for "The Pepsi Generation" and "for those who think young" is great imagery. But when your young-thinking endorsers are charged with such offenses as taking sexual liberties with a child or with rape, you want to distance yourself from the person as much and as quickly as possible, knowing too that there is a segment of the population that will also think badly of you for not supporting or standing by your endorser in a time of need. Run or stay—what do you do?

About the only quick and easy answer is to say that you will be waiting and watching with great concern to see how the process plays out and that you hope fairness and justice prevail. Then you wait to hear if your stockholders only want you fired or if they hope something more graphic befalls you.

The Florida Citrus Commission has also had some bumpy pickin' in its choices of celebrities Anita Bryant, Burt Reynolds and Rush Limbaugh as their various celebrity spokespersons over the years. Ms. Bryant, a one-time squeaky clean Miss Oklahoma beauty pageant winner, became a nationally-known singer and recording artist, spokesperson for Florida oranges and a national crusader against gay rights, in that order. Virtually every rally and appearance of hers was attended by a substantial contingent of vocal protesters and the national press, each time focusing considerable attention on her role as an endorser. As issues from her private life became public, the situation went from bad to worse. Mr. Reynolds became involved in a very ugly and public divorce and custody battle. Mr. Limbaugh, while not involved in a scandal, has been a lightning rod for critics and protests since his rise to prominence as a very colorful and vocal spokesperson for conservative political issues. His detractors tried to organize an orange juice boycott and to pressure Florida growers to sever their ties with Mr. Limbaugh. The growers professed their support of him, but did not renew his contract after the first year. The amount of publicity received was massive, but is it the kind of publicity that benefits Florida orange growers in the short or long term?

When it comes to illustrations of the crisis factor as a consideration involving celebrity endorsers, O.J. Simpson will surely be regarded as the textbook example. The football star turned sportscaster and actor had become a popular figure in advertising, lending his celebrity presence to spots for a number of companies and products including Powerhouse Sports Drink, MCI Communications, Playboy and his by-far most famous association, Hertz Corporation. The commercials featuring Mr. Simpson running through airports for Hertz Rent-a-Car became classics which even he himself would re-create in parodies for years. When Mr. Simpson was charged with murder in 1994 and became the focus of what the media termed "the trial of the century," the public held its breath, shock waves rippled and, in a cold pragmatic moment, business evaluated the repercussions of a high-profile, well-identified celebrity to the business he represented. Few stories about Mr. Simpson's troubles omitted his Hertz association. The company's initial reaction to the news clearly was panic, as it sought to distance itself from Mr. Simpson and suggest its connection to him was long over. This action was ultimately to be a greater embarrassment to Hertz.

The case was the subject of books, articles, videos and major news stories for more than a year, always with Hertz prominently mentioned. The advertising trade publication *Advertising Age* covered each phase along with the rest of the media, but with special interest to its implications for advertising and marketers. An editorial appeared under the headline "Sponsors can't hide" and took a hard look at responsibility by association. It noted " . . . Mr. Simpson's conduct raises new and unyielding questions related to how best to blend individual and corporate responsibilities when personal difficulties occur . . . No longer is it enough for marketers to state that their interests are protected by a simple morals clause in a contract that can be invoked if and when a celebrity's behavior leads to bad publicity. There's more to it."

Other industry headlines blared, "O.J. case casts pall on endorsers." Another asked, "What to do with a fallen star?"

The ultimate conclusion, of course, is that whatever the fates would have in store for Mr. Simpson, the Hertz Corporation and his other sponsors are forever footnotes in the story, another bold example of how any publicity is *not* good publicity.

Obviously, most celebrity endorsers will never be charged with murder and the subject of "the trial of the century." But this worst case situation supports the idea of not treating the celebrity endorser idea too casually.

But from a general perspective, the subject is still complex.

In a time of appealing anti-heroes and a global "stand-up and be counted" mood, perhaps engaging a celebrity endorser such as Rush Limbaugh, who is bold, controversial and even offensive to some segments of the audience, is the kind of image identification you believe will benefit you. If that's your choice, it is risky, but may very well be the step that helps you to "break from the pack" and gain greater differentiation and recognition. Be aware, though, that public opinion shifts and the sensational can become tiresome. Don't rely too heavily on short-term hits. Those represent publicity stunts, not marketing programs.

SPONSORSHIP

On a wider stage than the celebrity endorsement is the sponsorship. This, of course, can focus on the single endorser, as is the case when an advertiser will become the "official sponsor" of a performer's concerts and have a company or product name on everything from ads to tickets to signage to programs and merchandise. Visa was the sponsor of a Paul McCartney concert tour, Budweiser for the Rolling Stones, and so on. It is a rather grand way for a sponsor/advertiser to gain image identification with a performer's fans.

In other cases, the sponsor will go broader still and be the entity to present a summer concert series, theater season, golf or tennis tournament, ballet, ice show, or a single touring exhibition of art, history, culture or whatever translates to the most appropriate image-match for what it is you want to accomplish. Usually, despite the presence of possible other advertising, sponsorship means having your name as part of the actual event, such as:

- The Budweiser Triathlon
- Firestone 500

- Kemper Open
- Marlboro Grand Prix
- Philip Morris and The National Archives Celebration of the 200th Anniversary of the Bill of Rights
- Virginia Slims Tennis Tournament
- Volvo Tennis Tournament
- Toyota Comedy Festival
- JVC Jazz Festival

When resources permit, being able to emblazon "American Express Gold Card Events" on a broad list of concerts, plays and tournaments may blur the identification and image, unless the image you are seeking to create is one that the American Express Gold Card "is everywhere you want to be," the company's slogan.

Similarly, television and radio programs that have put the product name in the program title have sought to make a statement identifying the product or company with images from haughty to hip, such as:

- The Colgate Comedy Hour
- Dorito's Stand Up Stand Up
- The Hallmark Hall of Fame
- Kraft Music Hall
- The Voice of Firestone

Sponsorships don't all have to be on the level of Pepsi underwriting the Michael Jackson World Tour or the network television Bell Telephone Hour. They can be just as effective (in relative terms) for little more than a withdrawal from petty cash. A sponsorship of a local Little League team creates goodwill in a community, encourages loyalty, business referrals, and brings your name to the attention of some who may not have otherwise seen it. All the same benefits are possible from a local sponsorship of:

- a musical arts competition
- a bike race

- a marathon
- a fundraising event for a worthy cause
- any local sporting event
- an information and education program or series aimed at benefitting children or seniors
- a "health fair"
- a concert series of local musicians
- an exhibit of the works of local artists

A local public relations professional can help create a list of the potential opportunities for sponsorships. Again, using the marketing plan as a guide, determine who is your audience and what image you want to present to them. Finding a celebrity whose image is compatible or an event to put your name above are opportunities for short-cut image building. But be certain such steps are consistent with your objectives and your plan as such "shotgun" moves as an occasional ad or sponsorship are too quickly forgotten and create unrealistically high expectations. Identifying with an event, an issue or a cause as a sponsor, *purely* for *image* purposes can backfire and damage a reputation irreparably.

Sometimes ad agencies, in a subtle effort to ingratiate themselves with clients, will suggest you look no further than the executive suite for a spokesman, noting how Lee Iacocca, Ted Turner and Donald Trump, to name just three, acted as spokesmen for their respective entities and seemed to be well received. Remember again the eye of the beholder. From a distance of time, pundits still debate whether Mr. Iacocca's later appearances as a spokesman for Chrysler did not damage the goodwill he created in his earlier spots, and the other gentlemen have critics so vocal that their presence will always be viewed as overshadowing their message.

The simple truth is that not every CEO is a Charles Schwab or a Colonel Sanders. Chicken farmer–executive Frank Purdue was regarded as unintentionally funny in his commercial appearances and that's a pretty risky situation.

Even if your founder or CEO is articulate and photogenic, mixing the jobs of running a company and being a commercial presenter suggests one or the other position is not your "real job" and your audience deserves the best face you can put on your message. Show a photo of the CEO and perhaps quote him or her in a "mission statement" and leave the presentation to professionals who should be held accountable for the degree to which their performance is successful or not.

AT A GLANCE: THE UPS AND DOWNS OF ENDORSEMENTS AND SPONSORSHIPS

1. If the image you want is already personified by a particular celebrity, an association may help identify the celebrity with you and you with the image.
2. The three critical considerations in determining the wisdom of using a celebrity endorser are cost, credibility and the crisis factor.
3. The endorser should never be or become more important than the product. That is, an endorser should never upstage the product.
4. The celebrity's participation and identification should help achieve the objectives spelled out in the marketing plan.
5. The cost of the celebrity endorser should never be such a large percentage of the budget that production value and media suffer. Regardless of how effective the endorser, poor quality in production in any medium, and an insufficient opportunity to see the endorsement and its effects, is bad business.
6. Ads featuring recognizable people—people who already have a "following"—get earlier and greater attention and recall scores.
7. A celebrity endorser should not only be recognizable, but should be *influential*—have the ability to deliver an audience and persuade them to consider the marketed entity.

8. A check list should be developed that compares the celebrity endorser to an unknown actor or model in the same role, comparing attributes and liabilities.

9. A celebrity should have credibility as an endorser, and should not be overexposed through a myriad of endorsement deals.

10. A celebrity should not pose a high risk of attracting negative attention or involving the marketed entity in a potential scandal.

11. A celebrity should not alienate segments of the population.

12. Sponsorships should be chosen to reflect the attitude and image a person, product, company or service wants to present.

13. Sponsorships can be on a huge national or global scale or can be modest community relations-types of projects that project an image, yet return goodwill to the local community.

14. Avoid "shotgun" marketing programs, where advertising and promotion take a "hit and run" approach.

15. Big, splashy projects seem to be quickly forgotten.

Seriously Not Taking Yourself Too Seriously

We've come to understand that marketing encompasses a lot of elements—packaging, pricing, positioning, promotion—but it mostly deals in an overall sense with the process of *differentiating*. Getting a person, product, service or company noticed apart from its most direct or indirect competition is the goal. Advertising and public relations are, of course, the most obvious and consistently employed vehicles to achieve this.

Ask most anyone outside the profession what he or she thinks about advertising, and you can be fairly certain the response will come back, "There's too much of it."

That response is correct.

What is also correct is that the public has a love/hate relationship with advertising. It is often angrily dismissed as clutter—and intrusive clutter at that. It interrupts the flow of our reading, our listening, our viewing and even, in the case of billboards, our enjoyment of nature. Yet, many of our most successful magazines are purchased frequently for their advertising as well as for their editorial content, such as *Modern Bride, Harper's Bazaar, GQ* and any number of computer magazines. Understandably, people don't like admitting to this, but the response rate to ads proves their effectiveness and is why the media can continue to charge ever-increasing rates. Sunday newspapers are often heavy and cumbersome, loaded as they are with a wide variety of ad supplements and sale flyers readers eagerly await.

In evaluating ads, the words "dull" and "boring" are heard again and again. It would seem the very art of the process, not to mention the talents of a cadre of "creative directors," should make dull and boring the very last words people would apply. Alas, the dullness is largely a reflection of the *sameness* of so many ads. This is especially true when an ad is considered successful. Imitators abound, the very opposite response one might expect in a business so heavy with creative directors and creative departments. Too often, those who believe they have "studied with the masters" go on to imitate their work and answer criticism by saying it is an approach that worked before with tremendous success. Okay. So, now let's see something *else*.

One car company rather ingeniously broke with tradition and ran ads that did not show the car. Instead, the company sold *image*—how the car felt, the sensation one got from driving it. The campaign was interesting and successful enough that people actually went to the dealership to get a look at the car. So, before you could say "imitation is the sincerest form of laziness," other car companies began running ads that appeared poetic, dignified, even a bit smug . . . and which did not show the car. All type. Not even a graphic, much less a photo. The suggestion was that by this time everyone was familiar enough with what qualifies as a luxury car, a family car, an economy car or a sports car. Therefore, to *mention* any of these conjures up images that are perhaps even more vivid—and certainly less expensive—than showing the car itself. After all, we *have* seen cars before, and if the imagery can create a scene for us that is more dramatic than the one that might have been committed to film, then let the buyer be there. Zen had come to car advertising.

Some time ago, an astute marketer in the automobile industry said people give all types of reasons why they purchase the cars they do—all except the *real one*. Economy, fuel-efficiency, roominess, affordability are all swell, but the *real* reason most men and women choose the cars that they buy is based on the image of the car and the image of themselves—slick, sexy, successful or whatever the picture is they might have of themselves, whether in fantasy or reality. The car companies, being aware of this, go to the greatest lengths to name cars for that which best symbolizes the desired imagery:

Cougar	Crown Victoria
Mustang	Civic
Celebrity	Legend
New Yorker	Eagle
Riviera	Cherokee
Le Mans	Bronco
Grand Prix	Wagoneer
Towne Car	

These are just a few and these are just cars. We haven't touched on scents with names like Obsession, Passion, Brut, and Stud. No attempt has been made to suggest quality, economy, value or any other attribute that might offer a reason to buy. Except *image*. And when it comes to purchasing something people want to somehow represent their personality or status, what better way than imagery?

But when the imagery becomes so widely used as to seem almost universal—comparing an eagle to a mustang—what imagery then? Many marketers, opting for yet another point of differentiation: go for the laugh.

Most every public speaker, from statesman to CEO, knows that to relax an audience and "warm them up" one opens with a joke or a lighthearted reference. Humor in advertising has succeeded in differentiating people, products and companies thought not to be especially different from one another. Very often, humorous ads don't only register, they score huge successes. *Advertising Age*'s list of "The 50 Best Commercials" includes no less than 21 humorous spots. Humorous ads, promotions and identification have contributed mightily to building brands and brand images.

Much has been written about humor, and most of it isn't funny. Humor is difficult to analyze in a business sense because it is so subjective. Most humorists have an equal number of fans and detractors. Some people scream with laughter at the acerbic, insulting humor of Joan Rivers or Don Rickles. Others find their humor tasteless, rude or offensive. The list of comic writers and performers who have achieved success illustrates the point, from Buster Keaton to Woody Allen to Bob Newhart to Andrew Dice Clay to Richard Pryor and so many others, that different people find different things funny. So taking a humorous approach can be risky.

In the 1990s, "political correctness" narrowed the lines even more. Despite the wealth of comedic outlets, it was exceedingly more difficult for business to try "a lighter reference" without seeming to insult any number of minorities, professions or interest groups. But the idea of humor being used as a marketing device has long been the subject of some controversy. Advertising guru David Ogilvy wrote that

> Conventional wisdom has always held that people buy products because they believe them to be nutritious, or labor-saving, or good value for money—not because the manufacturer tells jokes on television. Claude Hopkins, the father of modern advertising thundered "people don't buy from clowns."
>
> I think this was true in Hopkins' day, and I have reason to believe that it remained true until recently, but the latest wave of factor-analysis reveals that humor can now sell. This came as a great relief to me; I had always hated myself for rejecting the funny commercials submitted for my approval.

Mr. Ogilvy waited for research to tell him that humor could be used effectively to help build brands and sell merchandise. Along the way, some of the most conservative of enterprises— banks, brokerage firms, insurance companies—have used humor effectively. Often the aim of their approach has been to foster an image that would set them apart from their respective industries, especially in industries perceived as up-tight and stodgy. The desired outcome has been that, despite being financial concerns, for example, their sense of humor would "humanize" them, suggesting that they might be nicer, friendlier and easier to do business with. Metropolitan Life Insurance Company has run television and print ads for several years featuring Snoopy and other characters from Charles Schulz "Peanuts" comic strip.

Still, Claude Hopkins' admonition that "People don't buy from clowns" bears keeping in mind. Using humor can be touchy. So many people are easily offended, and shareholders are inclined to be critical of anything that doesn't seem to be totally serious business when it comes to their money.

Twice-defeated candidate Richard Nixon was regarded as stiff and humorless throughout his entire public life. His appearance for only seconds on the network TV comedy show "Rowan & Martin's Laugh-In," where he delivered the line "Sock it to me" as a dancer in a bikini danced, before and after his appearance, made the viewing audience believe that Mr. Nixon had both a great sense of humor and confidence in himself as a person and candidate to risk such an undignified public display. Political candidates and office holders now routinely appear on television talk shows and deliver prepared jokes and bits and play musical instruments, all to show their friendly, good-natured, human side.

Research indicates that ads featuring music and humor are the most watched and best remembered. Any number of product attributes may go unnoticed, but for many years to come, smiles of recognition will appear when people hear:

"I can't believe I ate the whole thing."

—Alka Seltzer

"Where's the beef?"

—Wendy's

"Thank you for your support."

—Bartles & Jaymes

"Today the pits, tomorrow the wrinkles."

—Sunsweet Prunes

"I coulda' had a V-8."

—V-8 Vegetable Juice

"Take it off—take it all off!"

—Noxzema Shave Cream

"Who put eight great tomatoes in that little bitty can?"

—Hunt's

And then there were the "spokesmen"—Mr. Whipple, the Ty-D-Bowl Man, Manners the Butler, Morris the Cat, Spuds McKenzie, Brother Dominick, the Maytag repairman, among others—the fictional characters who became more recognizable than our neighbors, who were supposed to make us smile or snort while pointing out features of toilet bowl cleaners or copy machines. Others, like Mrs. Olsen, Juan Valdez and the Jolly Green Giant, weren't supposed to be funny, but, nonetheless became the subject of laughs in actual ads and parodies for years.

Satirist and comedian Stan Freberg was credited as the man who "virtually invented and refined the funny commercial." While there may be considerable debate about who actually "invented" funny commercials and when that happened, without question Freberg's influence has been significant. A man of many talents, *The New York Times* called him "the Ché Guevara of advertising." *Advertising Age* said "he has been called the father of the funny commercial—outrageous may be a better word." Whatever level of credit is due, Stan Freberg may be unique in his understanding of the sorts of things that make people laugh and what sells product. A lot of people are funny, many more *think* they're funny, but using humor in a costly mass medium to sell something is not like telling a joke at a party. There's more to it, and the stakes are a lot higher.

In his book *It Only Hurts When I Laugh,* Mr. Freberg describes one of his early experiences on behalf of Chung King, the best-known brand of packaged Chinese foods. He was asked to screen a series of TV commercials: "Each one, it turned out, was worse than the one before. Hard sell, followed by stupid sell."

One spot, for example, had an announcer interviewing a baby who gave the announcer a loud raspberry and sprayed animated saliva all over the announcer's face. When Mr. Freberg described the work to the client as "without a doubt some of the worst commercials I've ever seen," he went on to explain why they didn't work and criticized "the feeble attempts at humor." His observations were insightful, but more importantly, they were honest and simple. Why couldn't any of the managers of an entire ad agency notice? Because humor is such a personal matter, some people will conclude that they personally know what other people will probably think is funny.

Huh?

In this case, Freberg says, "The baby joke doesn't work because canned chow mein is not something you feed to babies. Humor has to be based somewhat on reality. An announcer just wouldn't ask a baby how he liked your product, so you've lost the audience immediately. And having the baby spit at the announcer was an instant turn-off."

After determining that even the ad agency didn't think the spots were funny, but thought the audience might, Mr. Freberg, exasperated, shared some truths: "That's the attitude that's responsible for all the advertising that doesn't work. . . . If you don't like an ad, why should anybody else? And who are 'they'? We're all consumers."

Think of the times you sat among people who were howling with laughter at some joke or performance and you didn't get it. Or the times you shared what you thought was a witty or hysterical observation only to be met with a blank stare.

Think of the times when a keynote speaker's failed ice-breaker joke only seemed to make the room grow colder. From our youngest years, we are taught that one of the best qualities a person can have is a sense of humor.

And the ability to laugh at ourselves.

And not take things *too* seriously.

John O'Toole, one of the legends of contemporary advertising, wrote, "Humor is an emotional response like love, anger, nostalgia, frustration, pride in achievement, and grief. Unlike them, however, it can be intellectualized to distinguish an "in-group" from an "out-group." That's what "camp" humor is all about, and it's why it will close up more prospects than it will reach when used in advertising.

"Moreover, humor being the complex social phenomenon it is—a catharsis, a release from tension—is often based on putting someone down, inflicting humiliation. The pie-in-the-face and the pratfall may be legitimate devices of show business, but in advertising they are going to get more people shaking their heads than nodding, more prospects sympathizing with the recipient of the pie than with the deliverer.

"The kind of humor to employ in advertising is the kind that demonstrates an insight into the human condition, one the advertiser shares with the prospect."

For a moment it was looking as if Mr. O'Toole had not yet seen David Ogilvy's research and was still buying Claude Hopkins' position. But John O'Toole came from a belief that advertising, marketing, telling your story, creating your image all represent serious propositions and should not be treated lightly. To try to represent yourself humorously seems more to contradict his belief than to find a place within it.

Without question, some comical ads have become textbook examples of both good advertising and good comedy. Alka-Seltzer and the Energizer bunny should be in the Hall of Fame. But the funny ad that works is the exception, not the rule.

Perhaps one of the best-constructed print ads using humor and addressing the qualities of effective advertising was largely unseen by the general public. It has been in trade magazines, mailers and in perhaps a half-dozen books on advertising. It is the gem from McGraw-Hill Magazines that shows the total embodiment of every sales rep's worst nightmare: the humorless, intimidating, demoralizing prospect—a middle-aged man seated with fingers of both hands knitted together in front of him, in a swivel chair at least as unexciting as he is. He regards his visitor with this chilling litany:

I don't know who you are.

I don't know your company.

I don't know your company's product.

I don't know what your company stands for.

I don't know your company's customers.

I don't know your company's record.

I don't know your company's reputation.

Now—what do you want to sell me?

More than forty years after its first appearance, this ad can still prompt a smile and a wince. It also raises the points that need to be addressed in fashioning an image to take to market.

It is truly admirable to not take one's self too seriously, to have a sense of humor and to wish to be thought of as witty with all the image of self-confidence that often accompanies wit. But ads that are created just to get laughs and to win awards—indeed, an *image* built largely on "going for the laugh"—lose sight of the objective, which should be in no small way to create and maintain an image that helps present you as a winner, whether you are selling dog food or running for Congress.

Consider, too, a dual problem with attempting to build an image on humorous ads. First, after hearing something funny a time or two, people tend not to find it funny anymore and tune-out sooner than to a straight message that focuses on just the right information.

Second, there is an expectation of those who become known for humorous ads that each successive ad will be at least as funny as the one that came before it. This puts limitations on the parameters involved in creating an image while raising steadily the expectations as the campaign attempts to build. It is easy to lose focus again on the objective in an attempt to consistently top yourself in the entertainment aspect of the ad.

Remember Hopkins' words, "People don't buy from clowns," and John O'Toole's belief that the best humor "demonstrates an insight into the human condition, one the advertiser shares with the prospect."

To that end:

- Don't undertake the task of creating an image, building an image or changing an image, by using humor as a substitute for a clear message that helps to define who and what you are and what you represent in terms of measurable value to your target audience.

- Don't insult people.

- Don't insult people's intelligence.

- Don't insult (however subtly) your competition.

- Don't create ads that risk offending or alienating segments of your target market.
- Take it easy and lighten up, but don't lose sight of the objective of your plan being to *market,* not just to get a laugh.

AT A GLANCE: SERIOUSLY NOT TAKING YOURSELF TOO SERIOUSLY

1. Marketing, in an overall sense, deals with the process of differentiating.
2. Advertising and public relations are the prime vehicles used to accomplish this.
3. The public has a love/hate relationship with advertising, believing there is too much of it, yet relying on it for information.
4. Many of the most successful magazines are purchased for their ads. Choose your media carefully.
5. Humor is difficult to analyze because it is so subjective. This is especially important to consider when considering presenting humorous ads.
6. It is extremely difficult in the 1980s to use humor in a way that does not offend some persons or group.
7. Even the most conservative figures and political candidates make it a point to appear on youth-oriented comedy programs to dispel images of stuffiness.
8. A lot of people are funny. Many more *think* they're funny. But using humor in costly mass media is not like telling a joke at a party. The stakes are a lot higher.
9. "Humor is an emotional response, like love, anger, nostalgia, frustration, pride in achievement and grief." (O'Toole)

10. "The kind of humor to employ in advertising is the kind that demonstrates an insight into the human condition." (O'Toole)
11. Don't use humor as a substitute for a clear message that helps define you and assist in your image-building efforts.
12. Don't insult people.
13. Don't insult the competition.
14. Take it easy; lighten up, stay focused on the goal of your marketing, not just getting people to laugh at your ads.

6

The Media and the Budget

What Should Image Marketing Cost?

Regardless of the image to be marketed, whether a career in professional services or in politics, a company or a service or a product, virtually no one has unlimited funds available, and to take the subject seriously means to treat it like a business expense or an investment. Those allocations are carefully considered and are part of a fixed budget.

The way image marketing is different from other line items in the budget is that it will likely straddle or overlap several lines and different stages will be funded at different times. There may be a line for advertising and even a specific budget for *image* advertising, but image *marketing* will likely encompass a good deal more than advertising. When considered from an image marketing perspective, however, components that might otherwise be independent of one another must all be interrelated.

An annual report should be—but isn't always—as important for the image it conveys as for the financial data it presents. It can be a colorless, black on white, no-frills document with all the sizzle of a prospectus. Or it can be costly, glossy and dramatic with

elaborate die-cuts, embossing, photography and enamel. Or anywhere in between. For generations, a number of financial institutions and financial services would seem to spare no expense when
it came to creating dazzling annual reports, while maintaining a
bland, conservative presence in every other respect. The rationale
was that the annual report was how investors and the financial
community judged an enterprise and, while it needed to convey a
certain sense of financial savvy, the piece would act as a corporate
brochure of sorts and needs to hold its own in a sea of high-gloss,
high-glitz annual reports. It became, in effect, an *image* piece,
albeit a stand-alone one. In an image marketing program, the
annual report may be exactly the same, but it will reflect and
reinforce elements that would be employed, elsewhere from signage
to letterhead, mailers, ads, catalogs, shipping materials, trucks,
vans and corporate neckties.

A financial institution in Chicago produced an annual report
that was the ultimate in understatement, plain and devoid of any
art or photography or graphics of any kind. The institution wanted
to tell its investors how carefully it watched its money and did not
want to appear to indulge itself on splashy printed pieces. Yet, its
offices, fully open to the public, were accented with magnificent
oriental rugs, rich wood paneling and furnishings worthy of the
most elegant private clubs. The overall image conveyed by this
contrast of images was that the institution's resources were available to indulge the tastes of management, while another message
was being offered to analysts. The net result was the appearance
of high spending and the absence of a management plan.

Public relations presents a wide range of options. Some entities put the entire PR budget into *government relations,* allocat-
ing it to a lobbyist or lawyer to try to influence legislators or
regulators, while otherwise maintaining a low profile. Others will
go in exactly the opposite direction and count on a high profile and
general public support to spill over and influence the regulators.
There is no correct way to do it, except to follow the strategy that
is consistent with the marketing plan to achieve defined objectives.

Media planning, whether through advertising, public relations or both, presents a varied menu from specialized trade and
industry publications to mass media broadcast appearances and
references.

THE MEDIUM AND THE MESSAGE: WHERE TO GO AND WHY

Much discussion includes phrases that allow how "the media this . . ." or "the media that. . .," usually suggesting a criticism of news coverage or characterizations. But what picture comes to mind when you hear the term *the media*? Is it a large group of people, perhaps thousands, all grouped together and writing with one pen or speaking with one voice?

Of course not.

Get straight about the media. While everyone brings his or her own sense of perspective to this discussion, who and what make up the media are extremely varied.

The print press includes *The Wall Street Journal* and the *National Enquirer*. If these two highly visible and aggressive national publications seem too extreme, consider that in a single American town, Washington, D.C., the two daily newspapers—the *Washington Post* and the *Washington Star*—could not be more dissimilar in editorial policy and perspective.

Magazines? Not too long ago thought to be an endangered species, magazines flourish. For every casualty to low circulation and ad deprivation, new titles appear in virtually every category—health and sports, entertainment, even specialty magazines for beer drinkers, wine lovers and cigar smokers.

The image meets the niche.

There are weeklies, monthlies and bi-monthlies for every taste, subject and demographic. *PC Week* is a leader in a category exploding with titles with no signs of declining interest as even *its* market develops its own group of subinterests; *Men's Journal* became an instant success from the publisher of *Rolling Stone* and *Us* magazines and, within months, imitators were launched to compete for shelf space and ad dollars. Despite the substantial expense of producing a national weekly magazine, the politically conservative weekly *The Standard* expected to succeed because its own principal editors and writers were high-profile political pundits and advisors seen as influential in their own right. They were exploiting their individual images and reputations to launch a new venture that would have its own image reflected by their collective strengths. *The New Yorker* maintains its historic image of sophistication and wit, while reflecting a contemporary sense of style and a reputation for offering superior examples of literature and the arts. Perennials, such as *Architectural Digest, Redbook, Cosmopolitan,* and *The Reader's Digest* continue to provide what their audiences want and expect, while gently stretching to appear fresh. The field is as fertile in the 1990s as at any time in publishing history, and each title offers an image of a stage on which marketers may present images of their own.

Television offers opportunities richer and more varied each year. On mainstream broadcast TV, besides several hours of national and local news each day, syndicated and cable programming ventures cover the most technical and intellectual offerings as well as the sensational, the stylish and the most esoteric forms of entertainment and sports. Advertising time is available full run or in selected "spot" markets. Product placements are the rule and no longer the exception.

So when a conversation includes the term *the media,* is the speaker today referring to *The New York Times,* "Hard Copy," "World News Tonight," "The McLaughlin Group" or "Entertainment Tonight"? It is a safe bet that any two of these stages would place, showcase or treat your story—from finance to show business to politics—quite differently.

Advertisers have found that the inclusion in ad reprints of a line such as "as seen in *The Wall Street Journal*" goes a long way in enhancing an image.

COMPETING FOR TIME AND SPACE

Andy Warhol said everyone would have his or her fifteen minutes of fame. Fame, of course, is a relative thing. The "Mona Lisa" is famous and timeless. The performer who enjoys a brief career, some reviews and recognition, for better or worse, experiences fame. So do the Little League team star, the Homecoming Queen, the winner of the race and the great-grandmother whose photo is seen on TV on her 100th birthday. And the impression that's made, creating perceptions, leaves a memory of an image.

The American culture in the 1990s is geared to the exploitation of individual moments. No longer is there a single, most dramatic memory of a trip, an accident or a special person or private remembrance. Modern times appear to demand that an accident victim, a member of the jury, a friend or a relative or neighbor of a star, a hero or a killer, sit for interviews and/or publish a book. Fame by association—for profit—is the order of the day. The result is a steadily blurring line regarding celebrity status, earned or rewarded. The public grants recognition to people, although it's not always certain why.

This poses unique challenges to marketers, advertising and public relations professionals who are seeking more than passing recognition for a person, product, service or company, competing for attention in a crowded tableau.

Public cynicism is rampant as well. A carefully orchestrated career in whatever field culminates on a national television show with an appearance, an interview and a public image being presented. In another segment of the same program, a witness to a hot air balloon accident, who happens to be a barber, is interviewed. The next day the barber shop is packed with customers and the barber is famous. The person who earned and deserved recognition in the first segment is on an equal level with the barber when it comes to public recognition. How each exploits the moment will determine who gets the sixteenth moment of fame. Some days it seems as if there is no justice in the world.

The serious marketer, hoping to create and develop an image that will help to support a larger marketing effort, must face an uphill battle for attention against news and clutter. The paid publicist works tirelessly to place a client on an interview program where other subjects may well be less worthy, but more colorful. Again, here is where the marketing plan must be relied upon to provide strategies and tactics that elevate the subject to stand-out proportions.

Competition for media time and space, whether arranged or purchased, is not merely intense, it is occasionally absurd. Preparing for such possibilities by projecting "worst case scenarios" is helpful.

MAKE THE MEDIA FIT YOUR IMAGE

Television is typically regarded as the medium with the broadest reach. It also carries the heftiest price tag against the media reaching audiences of comparable size.

Many public relations people have recommended "public access" cable television as a way of getting on TV, controlling the format and content of the presentation and securing visibility at virtually no cost. Experienced business people and sensible twelve-year-olds usually notice that something that costs nothing is rarely worth more than that.

The Federal Communications Commission has, in its wisdom, historically required television stations to do a certain amount of public service programming. These are the shows that television has broadcast regularly on Saturday and Sunday mornings between 5 A.M. and 6:30 A.M. Announcements of school closings and earthquakes may also be counted as public service time when license renewals come around. Cable television operators, in order to be granted a franchise for a given area, not only promise to make public service announcements, but to dedicate a channel on the cable system for full public access. Any member of the public may reserve a parcel of time and present a tape for airing. It can be a talk show, film or music reviews or any presentation that might have previously been reserved for a corner of the park.

By the mid-1990s, the "programming" on most public access television channels looked much like cheesy kitchen table programs. In this respect at least, "Wayne's World" is a more accurate reflection of reality than one might think.

Being allowed the air time—or cable time—to present whatever you want is only a small part of the program. Yes, it is cheap, but without an audience, much less a demographically disposed-to-your-message audience, having your own 24-hour channel doesn't count for much. You may as well talk to your mirror and save the cost of film or tape.

Whether your media presence is in the form of a paid advertisement or commercial spot or an appearance on a program for which you did not have to pay to appear, consider the time, place and format wisely. Just as it is not true that "any publicity is good publicity," and *where* you deliver a speech is as important as the speech itself, so too does it matter where your media appearances are. Hopefully, they will not be a random appearance, but a step in the process of creating the awareness and overall image that is your objective. Appearing in the wrong format, time and place is to be avoided, as tempting as it may appear to be.

In *Power and Influence* Robert L. Dilenschneider notes "Effective marketing influence means reaching consumers at their most receptive moment."

That can mean advertising on the Super Bowl, the local morning or evening news or, as Mobil Oil learned from the tremendous impact it registered over the years, from a single sentence spoken on the Public Broadcast System: "Masterpiece Theater is brought to you by a grant from the Mobil Oil Corporation." No commercials, no pictures of gas pumps, trash bags or travel guides. Just that one line, delivered with maximum economy and understatement, created years of goodwill. Despite rising fuel prices and, for a time, long lines at service stations and an absence of actual "service," Mobil was one oil company that had created the image of an American company with interests in every neighborhood, bringing culture and a touch of class into every home at least once each week.

But a grant to PBS is a bit of a stretch for many ad budgets. Even a grant to the local PBS station may seem to provide little in the way of a trade-off. The essence of a PBS connection is to exploit the "grant" to maximum benefit. As with sponsorship of a cause, from a business standpoint, the marketing value is in having your participation well publicized. Even the smallest contribution or grant should be noted in print materials and as a tag line in ads and point of sale displays.

Cable TV has not only changed the way people watch television, but it has altered the promise of television as an ad medium. Advertising agency people will tell you that because of cable TV, you can now afford to run ads on TV, a medium once thought to be outside the reach of most smaller advertisers. That's true and false. It is cheaper to advertise on most cable channels than on most broadcast channels because of the comparative size of the audience. It is cheaper to advertise on The Fishing Channel than

on NBC, because The Fishing Channel only has about one percent
of NBC's audience at any given time. But if your company is a
maker of fishing boots, your dollar is likely going to produce a far
greater return for you on The Fishing Channel anyway.

In seeking a defined image to project, one previously had to
pretty much take whatever the networks and local programs offered—with the news and "family" programming being generic
ground for advertisers. In more modern times, of course, we know
MTV delivers the young audience; VH-1, the older end of the MTV
crowd; Lifetime is the Women's Channel; and, in addition, there's
BET (Black Entertainment Television) and any number of foreign
language channels. This proliferation has not only cut down on
both cost and "waste" in an advertiser's target audience, but the
proliferation of specialty channels has increased the number of
choices. There are now even more than one science, news, entertainment news, sports and weather channel from which to choose
and with which to negotiate.

Don't bother negotiating unless the image of the cable channel
fits your own image. Politicians who say they will go anywhere to
get their message out might do well to avoid the science fiction
channel or the cartoon channel. Appearances on religious channels
and home-shopping formats have helped guests sell philosophy,
political programs, and any amount of merchandise. Among the
most watched cable channels that conduct interviews, profile people
and companies, and accept advertising (from quick ads to infomercials) are:

CNBC
USA Network
EWTN—Eternal Word Television Network
America's Talking
VH–1
MTV—Music Television
Lifetime
TNN—The Nashville Network
The Family Channel

Comedy Central
Headline News
CNN—Cable News Network
Sports Channel
ESPN—Entertainment and Sports
E!—Entertainment Television
BET—Black Entertainment Television
A & E—Arts & Entertainment

And more channels are introduced all the time to appeal to the audience's more special interests. The problem with this proliferation of channels is not just that an ad budget can be stretched only so far, but so can an audience. As the audience totally and demographically gets cut up smaller and smaller, ratings will determine who survives. The idea of a 500-channel television system seems impressive from a high-tech standpoint, but since all but a few cable channels rely on advertising, the dream is economically unrealistic. With fewer than 10 channels, the dearth of material is visible. Further, to have a library of 500 books or records or CDs available whenever you need or want to use them is supportable, but 500 or so TV channels takes a major readjustment in how people live, learn and use such a resource. In short, the dramatic increase in the number of media choices available means a diffusion of audience.

The bad news is that advertisers must approach cable either warily or with eyes wide open to the status of cable programming at any given point in time. The good news is the recognition of this has forced cable channels to keep advertising rates comparatively low. More good news is that, while the general interest channels carry much of the off-network reruns that may not show impressive ratings numbers, the specialty channels, such as ESPN, TNN or BET, offer as finely tuned a demographic target, as their print counterparts.

In a public relations sense, to be interviewed or profiled on one of these special interest outlets is to be seen and heard by a smaller, but better qualified prospect for your message than the bigger-numbered broadcast networks that provide waste.

THE THEATER OF THE MIND

Radio is cable TV without the pictures—a variety of formats and specialty niches, most all of which have only a relatively small audience.

Bob Schulberg, Western Marketing Director for CBS Radio for more than 20 years, noted

> The generally accepted system of buying radio time is flawed. Quantitative measurements designed for television are too often uncritically adapted for radio. The system forces the buyer to see radio time as a commodity whose price is the only significant differential. It forces reliance on minute quantitative variances in audience data generated by ratings systems that are less than totally reliable. It takes absolutely no recognition of standard statistical error. Its presumption is that every radio listener is the same which is patently false.

Schulberg's point suggests that the numbers we rely on to gauge audience size are far less relevant than the actual make-up of the numbers—the qualitative as opposed to quantitative.

Historically, radio has been relegated to the status of background music or accompaniment to an activity, rather than a primary focus of attention (as is the case with TV and print). Yet, radio should not be taken for granted. The tremendous success of Rush Limbaugh, considered by many to be enormously influential in marshalling huge numbers of people both for and against any number of causes, cannot be underrated. From an image marketing standpoint, an appearance, mention or endorsement by Mr. Limbaugh on his daily nationally syndicated radio program can go a long way to defining an image among his millions of loyal and devoted listeners. Similarly, the "Larry King Show," syndicated by the Mutual Radio Network, proved to be a powerful platform nationally for promoting books, films, candidates and points of view.

It is significant that upon leaving office, Senator Gary Hart and Governors Jerry Brown and Mario Cuomo became hosts of radio programs, believing the medium, with its high level of intimacy, served best to maintain their respective images and the opportunity to influence public opinion and perceptions. Likewise, former candidates for public office Ross Perot and Oliver North used radio talk programs as their way of staying close to their publics and nurturing a grassroots image.

The debate over which medium—print, TV, radio or out-of-home—is most effective will be an ongoing one and rightly so. The right medium must be determined within the framework of your marketing plan relative to your objective and your budget.

To achieve the image you want, consider the importance also of *ruling out* certain media for reasons other than budget. For example, Walter Winchell had the image of a crusading news reporter in his newspaper column and on his radio program. His attempt to transfer his strong, patriotic image to television failed as his rumpled appearance and affectations seemed cartoonish. Paul Harvey, the most consistently prominent, recognizable and respected figure in radio journalism for decades, found his expansive and expressive inflections and gestures—so much a successful part of his radio programs—curiously out of place and ill-suited to TV. Brilliant in his essays, magazines and his many books and novels, Truman Capote found that people did not respond well to him in broadcast interviews. His slight build, lisp and eccentric manner created an image that did not seem to fit the deep, soulful, insightful personality represented on the page.

Since the 1980s, political candidates' handlers have been increasingly concerned about a candidate's "negatives." Current polling methods take into account not only a candidate's name recognition and level of public approval, but what percentage of those polled admit to an overt *dislike* of anything or everything about the candidate. Just as it is freely acknowledged that good "word-of-mouth" advertising is the best kind to have, *bad* "word-of-mouth" advertising can be just as contagious. Such "negatives" are equally disturbing when the subject of the marketing effort is a product, service, or company. What makes it seem even worse is that people admitting to negative feelings can't always give a specific reason why. Someone may be the subject of a media "investigative" piece, without any actual charge of wrongdoing being put forward, yet weeks or months later, people might remember "having heard something bad" about the subject.

To this end, an important part of image marketing is the initial creation of a *reservoir of goodwill,* that can be drawn upon if and as needed at later times. Your marketing plan should include a strategy that addresses this issue specifically and advertising, public relations and promotional tactics to implement such a strategy.

The budget?

First, the research: To create a reservoir of goodwill, is there an obstacle to overcome? Is there negative opinion of your company, product, service, your industry or of you, yourself? Or are you relatively unknown or considered an underdog in your profession or industry? A portion of the cost of your *image marketing* effort is in your research.

Obviously, there will have to be a very different—and more costly—effort to *change* an image than to create one, although the task is rarely unachievable.

In such "turnaround" challenges, not only is a larger budget called for, but typically more time is required. Usually. Chapter 5 offered an example of former President Nixon, regarded as stiff and humorless, appearing on the TV show "Rowan and Martin's Laugh-in" and on "The Tonight Show," where he joked and played the piano. Either of these appearances would have done his cause some good, but *both* significantly changed many people's perception of him.

Conversely, when securities industry figure Michael Milken was convicted of fraud, his attempt to influence public opinion and the *judge* by taking underprivileged children to a baseball game was pretty transparent. He totally insulted the public with his gross underestimation of its ability to see through a very uncreative and cheap stunt.

Candidate Bill Clinton, while being publicly trashed amidst charges of "womanizing," agreed on the eve of an important primary election vote to appear on the TV show "60 Minutes." He discussed his problems with what appeared to be candor. While there was no flat-out admission of wrongdoing, Mr. Clinton, with his wife at his side, said he wasn't perfect and perhaps had done some things in his private life he regretted. Who hasn't? But for whatever anyone would say of him, he stated that he was satisfied that he was of good moral character—and his wife was there to agree with him (and squeeze his hand on camera from time to time). Whether one likes or believes Mr. Clinton is irrelevant. The TV appearance was very effective as it presented a man who did not hide or dismiss questions or offer an implausible story. The public reacted positively as it perceived he was showing courage in facing his accusers, a media which was itself distrusted.

Such appearances are not without risk. Senator Edward Kennedy's presidential campaign went down in flames when the senator seemed to virtually fall apart in front of the nation in a tense TV interview with reporter Roger Mudd.

Bill Clinton speaks well, thinks fast and knows how to use television effectively. A doctor, lawyer, judge, teacher or a corporate CEO may have the same excellent public speaking skills, a quick mind and an easy manner. Or not. And if not, it requires the advice of a coach on how to present oneself on television, while under fire and under pressure without appearing evasive or sinister. A public relations professional, engaging in some role playing, could ask questions of the worst kind to prepare you for the worst time. Reviewing both what you say and how you say it, paying attention to incidentals like clothing and hairstyles, seating angles and gestures and video taping the sessions to make you more comfortable with the camera and your own presentation are standard. The cost involved in such situations—to prepare and be comfortable and effective in media appearances—will vary depending on the amount of time the subject needs to prepare. It could be a couple of hours or many sessions over several days. Typically, such a situation is not a part of a standard PR budget.

So how should it be financed?

1. With funds from the PR budget?
2. From an education and training budget?
3. From contingency funds set aside in the budget for special situations?
4. From the budget of whatever department's story is the subject of the presentation?

Yes.

The next step is to merchandise what you have. Whatever the subject, if it is worth the CEO's time, it should be utilized in any or all the following ways:

1. An article in, or special issue of, a newsletter (sent to any number of constituents including employees, shareholders, regulators and the media).
2. A press release.
3. A position paper—explaining and/or taking a position on any subject of relevance to your constituent groups.
4. An "open letter" ad in a local paper where you take a very public position.

In the most traditional sense, the cost of image marketing should be represented as subcategories on budget items for:

Advertising

Public Relations

Promotions

Events, Grants, and Awards

Education and Training

Publications

Legal Affairs

Research and Development

Exhibits and Displays

What *percentage* of each item will be dedicated to image marketing will vary from issue to issue. But, clearly, it needs to be regarded as a factor in budget planning and allocation.

In each area, with the exception of advertising and public relations, funding for image marketing should not increase or change significantly the marketing budget. It may alter the allocation of dollars a bit, but image marketing should be regarded as a *way* to market, not an addition or alternative to marketing. It reflects a commitment to incorporate your image goals in virtually every component of your marketing program.

Advertising and PR, while reflecting image marketing concerns like other line items in the budget, have ultimately the most significant influence in determining what people think of you and how people think of you.

While at various times most everyone will have helpful suggestions as to where you should (or must!) allocate your media budget, there are 24 primary alternatives in eight basic categories under media. The eight are:

1. Newspapers
2. Magazines
3. Television
4. Radio
5. Outdoor
6. Out-of-home
7. Direct mail
8. Customized specialties

Separately and together, these are not only places to put your advertising, to generate awareness, visibility, perhaps even sales, but each is a platform with the potential to create or reinforce an image. There is a certain "image association" by advertising on ESPN, BET or MTV, for example. While the standard line is that all classifications may not be right for all entities, that doesn't apply here. Used in combination, as the budget permits, all together or with a single focus in any one area, effective image marketing is possible. Within these eight areas are:

1. daily newspapers including Sunday
2. weekly newspapers
3. community newspapers
4. national magazines
5. specialty or trade papers
6. general interest magazines
7. business magazines
8. trade magazines and newsletters
9. privately published/sponsored magazines
10. network television
11. local VHF and UHF television

12. cable television
13. satellite TV "superstations"
14. radio
15. billboards
16. transit advertising
17. waiting rooms and shelters
18. point of sale displays
19. signage and posters
20. direct marketing/direct mail includes telemarketing
21. in-flight advertising includes audio, video and print (magazines and catalogs)
22. video tapes—your own exclusive showcase or a co-op or the incorporating of your message into someone else's tape
23. uniqueness in packaging includes folders, wrappers, boxes, vehicles
24. novelties and specialty promotions and items, including note pads, caps, shirts

Each of these 24 options has break-outs and subcategories of their own. For example, newspapers in most markets have free-standing magazines, pull-out sections and inserts at least weekly. Often, these sections have the potential of having a longer shelf-life or pass-along than the newspaper itself. In some organizations, point number 24 (novelty and specialty promotional items) might be funded through the budget for special promotions, merchandising or collateral pieces, rather than an advertising budget. It doesn't matter what managers and accountants agree to call it, just as long as it gets done.

Infomercials—paid program-length TV commercials—pose another complex issue. They run, on average, just under 30 minutes. Even with a separate production budget, then, the cost of running a 30-minute infomercial will be substantial.

Additionally, the most consistently visible infomercials tend to represent one of two extremes when it comes to production value, and those extremes tend to define the genre in the public's mind. Infomercials either display a rather distracting and intrusive amount of techno-graphics and a well-rehearsed audience, or they are simply tedious and boring, yet suggesting the audience should be excited. This excitement is typically expressed by shouting. The overall low-budget look of most infomercials (two chairs, a table and a plant) make the viewing of Uncle Clarence's home movies seem like an artistic experience by comparison.

Of course, producers of infomercials would loudly protest such criticism, citing the vehicle's enormous success. That certainly is a point well taken. Infomercials probably deserve a volume to themselves. Considering the airwaves and cable channels are flooded with both infomercials and a plethora of home shopping channels—many of them doing very well or at least turning a profit—while the audience overall still complains about having to endure two or three-minute commercial interruptions to programming, the relative success of infomercials is surprising. The term *relative* is important here because not every infomercial is a success at moving huge amounts of product. What they *are* is often cheap, hence the low production quality. And infomercials themselves offer what appear to be commercials within.

Still, without question, there are certainly people who watch and respond to infomercials, just as from time to time, works of debatable merit have found success in every branch of the arts, thus prompting proponents to claim it is a worthy form.

Truly, image opportunities exist here, but the major issue is, to put it delicately, whether or not you *want* the kind of image that comes from identification with this form.

While the Federal Communications Commission requires that certain warnings and disclaimers be presented clearly, some viewers who come upon the infomercials think they are watching an actual program and that statements and claims offered are governed by the usual standards and ethics that traditionally governed what goes on television. These viewers constitute a minority, however, and most of the public knows that time and space have been purchased and the entire project—applause, agreements and expressions of amazement included—is all part of the script. Still, there is a certain surreal quality about the infomercial. The talk show format, the product demonstration for a cheering audience, the sharing of "secrets" of success, be it hair replacement, weight loss or the keys to awakening the giant within you, are all presented in such a way as to suggest genuine spontaneity. Yet, the revelation, the response and the crowd reaction are all written, rehearsed, taped, re-taped and edited.

Creating a positive and lasting image that breeds goodwill and loyalty requires sincerity, honesty, and integrity. The infomercial by its very nature presents an advertiser who, in choosing this format, has decided to be less than candid in offering a message, product or other entity.

Proponents say infomercials are entertainment in what are program-length commercials. Critics say they are not; rather that they are commercials masquerading as programs, trying to somehow deceive an unsuspecting public.

So, if so much of the public is wise to the concept and doesn't really believe all it sees and hears, why is there a long line of enterprises waiting to get their infomercials on the air?

Apart from the obvious answer that there are a number of enterprises who are less than honorable and don't have a problem with "fudging" a little on honesty and integrity, make a deal, take the money and run, there are a couple of theories. One theory is that, over the years, hit television programs such as "Saturday Night Live" and "SCTV" have produced so many parodies of commercials, interview shows and audience-participation shows that the public simply considers a staged routine pitching of a product to a fake audience "campy"—just more show business. Another theory is that people simply *expect* television to exaggerate, inflate and make things appear more dramatic than they are. Certainly TV news shows that have faked truck explosions and restaged actual news events for their cameras haven't done much to negate this theory. Another theory is that the public just doesn't care. With the heightened interest in catalog, mail-order or other shop-at-home devices, some members of the public will likely view infomercials as just one more way to view and call-in an order for a hairpiece, exercise equipment or a memory course.

To some advertisers, this is merely a throwback to the time when sponsors bought thirty, sixty or ninety minutes of TV time and presented whatever they wanted as the vehicle to showcase products. The difference, of course, is that legitimate drama, news or comedy was the actual centerpiece around which the product and messages or causes were touted.

This harangue against infomercials does not suggest that they are not effective selling vehicles. It is to suggest if the subject of your marketing effort is concerned about creating, maintaining or changing a public image, the infomercial itself carries such a controversial image that more reputable vehicles are recommended.

Among other options within the list of options might include *signage and posters* (point number 19), buttons and bumper stickers. This extremely simple, relatively inexpensive promotional subcategory has been the almost exclusive province of political campaigns for decades, after expanding into the somewhat passé luggage stickers territory in the 1950s. The family car touted clues about what and where the choice vacation and tourist spots were. By the 1970s and 1980s, bumper stickers and buttons invited observers to "Ask me about good health" and proudly signaled participation in causes (M.A.D.D.—Mothers Against Drunk Driving," "Just say no!") and saluted favorite cities ("I love [heart] New York"), sports teams and radio stations. It was no incidental feature that many of these stickers would also feature a "Pepsi" or other product or corporate logo. Many of the same children who might have received free school book covers from a friendly Prudential Insurance agent in the 1950s were, by the 1980s, driving cars with an "I own a piece of the rock" bumper sticker. This was proof that not every advertising vehicle that engenders goodwill and is seen and remembered has to cost a large amount. Further, a person who would wear a button or affix a bumper sticker to his or her car is making a major statement of endorsement, acceptance, approval and loyalty in the most blatant, yet understated way. Extensions of other options that cross media lines include coupons, membership cards, V.I.P./frequent user/bounce-back or discount cards, and stickers or stamps. All convey an image, a sense of participation.

The correct amount or percentage of a marketing budget to allocate for any particular options or for image marketing will be as different as the various marketing subjects, objectives, strategies and tactics as well as the budgets themselves.

A professional services practice or entity, for example, will likely allocate a larger percentage for community and public relations and for highly visible philanthropic endeavors than for traditional advertising programs. Consider, from an image marketing perspective, even in the 1990s, that the practice of advertising had been widespread among doctors and lawyers for more than a dozen years. Yet, many in those professions (and much of the general public) continued to think that advertising of this type was undignified.

Alternative marketing approaches more appropriate to such professions will be explored in a later chapter, but for purposes of budget considerations, the strategy and the tactics outlined in the marketing plan should consider that public service posters, flyers, newsletters and participation on boards and committees raise visibility and cost relatively little. Where the funds are available, endowing a chair, contributing to a building fund for a hospital, school, center for seniors or children or even a modest scholarship named for the benefactor and acknowledged in signage, press releases and an on-going marketing communications program (with mailings and newsletters) can be every bit as effective as a traditional advertising campaign and is likely to be more favorably regarded by conservative segments of an audience as more dignified. Since professional service groups typically have modest marketing budgets (if they have a marketing budget at all), this approach is likely to have a longer "shelf life," that is, maintain its influence longer.

Traditional advertising, however, should not be dismissed by marketers in favor of the trend of the moment. A solid, formula ad campaign presented in the right media with enough consistency will always outdo a quick hit for the impression it creates. An inclination is to equate doing something differently with doing it better or more powerfully. That's certainly not inherently the case. Calvin Klein, Apple Computer and Nike are three companies who have presented ads that were bold, different and memorable. They helped to position the companies within an image context. Others who have used ads that shocked people, Benneton, for example, have been talked about for their shock value as merely shocking ads and did little to advance the image of the company or its products.

So-called "cutting edge" ads that attempt to look like cable's hip, youth-oriented MTV, frequently offer rap music, jumpy hand-held camera work and people talking in sentence fragments. These ads seek to create a look of ultra-hipness.

Well.

Advertising on MTV with commercials that look like MTV is hardly the ultimate in creativity or imagination. Running the same ad elsewhere frequently looks like a contrived attempt at an MTV-like ad. Such pseudo-hipness passing for creativity, with one ad looking like another only adds to the clutter and does little to define the image of the advertiser. The right message with benefits to the viewer, wrapped in imagery targeted via the right media will succeed, if history can be believed. Knock-offs of trendy ads typically fail.

With budgets increasingly tighter in almost every market cycle, marketing dollars have to go farther and work harder. If TV is the only medium in the plan, wrap the message in strong, memorable imagery that supports who and what you want to be remembered for. An emotional pitch that ends with an invitation is stronger than a loud hard-sell pitch that tries to pack all of the information into a thirty-second TV spot. Newspaper ads with wall-to-wall type don't get read. Offer imagery and an invitation. Don't try to bowl people over with an ad.

Every ad in all media, regardless of the budget, should devote a *larger* percentage of time or space to the presentation of image— a memorable, emotional message—than to product, service or statistical data.

Product pitches are forgotten and are often heavy with information comparable to that of others. Factoids and footnotes required by the legal department may be required, but they are still largely irrelevant as they still won't keep you from getting sued if you're lying.

Images are remembered.

In *Marketing Corporate Image: The Company as Your Number One Product,* James R. Gregory offers that "image marketing is a burgeoning business, with more than half of the larger U.S. companies using advertising to promote ideas as well as products."

Well, what's good enough for "half of the larger U.S. companies" should be a lesson for at least that many enterprises of lesser net worth. But it should not be limited to only image *advertising* but should include the other marketing options, such as PR, direct mail, catalogs, sales promotions, public speaking and whatever ideas the strategy and tactics of your marketing plan devise.

Whatever the budget, the positioning of your enterprise—be it person, product, service, company or cause—must reflect some sense of your image at every level and every stage. To reflect such image considerations should not alter your existing budget appreciably, if at all.

AT A GLANCE: THE MEDIA AND THE BUDGET

1. Image Marketing straddles and overlaps several line items in a budget.
2. Different stages of marketing plans are funded over time—even over several budget periods and several years. Image Marketing follows this process.
3. Image should be reflected and reinforced in all elements of a program from signage to letterhead, mailers, ads, catalogs, shipping materials, trucks, vans and corporate items.
4. Understand the diversity of the media. It is not only the difference between TV and print, but between *TV Guide* and *The Wall Street Journal*. Choose media that reflects, supports and enhances your image.
5. "Fame by association" is a reflection of a media frenzy in the 1990s.
6. Inexpensive media opportunities, such as cable "access" channels, can promote an image of low quality and little value.
7. Effective marketing influence means reaching consumers at their most receptive moment.
8. Don't waste time even trying to negotiate a good advertising rate with a cable channel—or, for that matter, any media—if it does not reflect the image to which you aspire or are trying to maintain.

9. Saying you will "go anywhere" to get your message out, can be a huge mistake, if the media option will not only not advance your effort, but perhaps diminish it.

10. Whether in advertising or public relations, presence on a special-interest cable TV channel will reach a smaller, but more demographically qualified audience less expensively.

11. Radio is increasingly more influential in helping to create an image in certain segments of the market.

12. Eliminate certain media from consideration for reasons other than budget. Some people just don't present well in audio or video. Others may be charismatic in person or in video, but not strong in print. Qualify your best media options.

13. Create a reservoir of goodwill in your industry and community to enhance your image.

14. Determine what, if any, media may be utilized to help overcome negative aspects of your image.

15. Prepare for interviews with role-play situations. Video tape and review your presentation and mannerisms.

16. Merchandise your appearances and presentations as a means of enhancing your image. Create an article or newsletter as a vehicle to reprint an interview or a speech; send it to shareholders, the media and other constituents; adapt it to a press release, position paper or "open letter" ad in a local newspaper or trade magazine.

17. Typically, the funding of an Image Marketing effort should be spread over several budget line items including advertising, PR promotions, events, grants, awards, education, training, publications, legal affairs, research and development, recruiting, exhibits and displays.

18. Image Marketing should be considered as budgets are being prepared. What percentage of any given program's cost must be determined issue by issue.

19. Media opportunities for advertising lie in eight categories, with 24 main subcategories. Choose which best support your visibility and carry the most power to influence and inform.

20. Infomercials are popular and controversial. They are often quite effective, but consider carefully if they offer the kind of image you want.

21. So-called "cutting edge" advertising is often just a falling-in-step with a trend of the moment. If it's not a good fit, forget the trend of the moment and stay with the formula approach that's usually dependable.

22. An emotional pitch that ends with an invitation to call, write or come in for more information is a stronger message than a loud, hard-sell pitch that tries to pack all the information into a 30-second TV spot or a print ad with wall-to-wall type.

23. Every ad in all media should devote a larger percentage of time or space to imagery than to product, service or statistical data.

24. Product pitches are forgotten; images are remembered.

25. The positioning of the subject of the marketing effort must reflect some sense of your image at every level and every stage. To do so should not appreciably raise budgets if they are correctly prepared initially.

CHAPTER 7

When the Product Is Bigger than a Breadbox

How much should someone be able to tell about you by the image you present? That question was the basic premise of a television quiz show that people found interesting enough that it was asked every Sunday evening for seventeen years. The show, "What's My Line?," ran from 1950 to 1967 on CBS-TV. Mostly average-looking people would sit at a desk answering questions about whether or not they were tap dancers, glassblowers, county sheriffs, country doctors or CEO of a company that made cannonballs. To emphasize the importance of the questioning and the dignified nature of the whole business, the questioners were the best-dressed in the game show field. The women wore evening dresses and the men wore tuxedos. This very example of how seriously the program took itself helped to give it a high-class image.

Millions of people watched each week and played along with the panel, trying to determine on the basis of appearance, tone of voice, projection of confidence, friendliness, arrogance or sophistication, whether or not this person, regardless of occupation or profession, projected an image of being sneaky, trustworthy or simply *nice* and what he or she represented in the world of commerce or industry.

In one episode panelist Steve Allen, the author-composer-entertainer, addressing the matter of the product involved in the person's business or profession, asked a question that was to become as common as wondering if it were animal, vegetable or mineral. The question was, "Is it bigger than a breadbox?"

While those at the threshold of the twenty-first century may debate whether or not young people have any idea what a breadbox is, marketers then and now recognized how that question spoke volumes about the product's marketing options.

No bigger than a breadbox—barely larger than a standard size loaf of bread—meant that changes in packaging, warehousing, distribution, shipping, delivery and service were likely possible with a certain flexibility and manageable cost. *Bigger* than a breadbox suggested fewer manageable or affordable marketing options.

And what if the product—and to marketers, whether the subject is a person, place, thing, issue, cause or life itself, it is defined as the *product*—is a *lot* bigger?

What if the product is, for example, an entire industry or profession, a city, a country, a political or social issue? Or an entertainer or a candidate for public office?

By almost anyone's standards, these "products" are most certainly bigger than a breadbox.

Some professions have historically rejected—and even *resented*—marketing in general and advertising in particular. The often-heard complaint has been that the idea of selling the services of a doctor, lawyer, accounting or consulting firm "like a box of laundry detergent" was not only undignified, but totally demeaning to the profession. Of course, time and laundry detergents have changed and, while many professions had to be dragged kicking and screaming to articles or seminars on marketing, the practice is now, for better or worse, a part of the business plan. Virtually every business, to survive, depends on getting *new* business—and new business comes from marketing efforts.

A generation ago, public utilities advertising was service-oriented. Military recruiting ads (about the only ads the military ran) had not progressed a great deal from the "Uncle Sam wants you" posters of a half-century ago. And, of course, any advertising by doctors, lawyers or religious denominations and their individual churches, was simply unimaginable. As for public images, the culture itself sustained and supported them over the years. They were simply an accepted part of America's everyday life and a very important prestigious part at that. To become a doctor, a lawyer, a member of the clergy or an officer in a branch of the armed services was to become a part of the country's elite.

MARKETING THE MILITARY

When young men turned eighteen, they registered with their local draft boards and could expect to be called for military service within a couple of years. If they chose to become a Marine or wanted to be in the Navy or Air Force, enlistment was an option. The benefits were fairly well known as they were similar to what they had been for generations. In any case, the culture—the simple established system of how things were done—supported the process. Should there be a moment of doubt or hesitation, Hollywood films reminded and promised that a stint in "the military" meant honor, duty, strength of character and a lot of colorful, memorable stories to one day share with one's grandchildren.

The Vietnam conflict, which created such enormous division within the country, most dramatically affected the image of the country's military services. Years after the conflict, with the draft abolished, an all-volunteer military and largely peacetime conditions, military service was no longer a "duty," but viewed as a choice and to a segment of the population, a dubious one. Such thinking is part of the legacy of the social and cultural revolution that began in the United States in the 1960s and continued into the 1970s. The discipline and tradition in service that was the rule now finds those who make application to participate petitioning, demonstrating, protesting and regularly suing for changes and accommodations in what are now frequently successful attempts to change the structure of the most historic institutions.

In the case of the military services, always the definition of comradery, in a David-and-Goliath posture, military personnel are characterized more as bullying and heavy-handed than as disciplined and efficient. The concept of discipline, regulation and adherence to orders without question—has been questioned. And the resulting accommodation, whether by agreement or legal action, has left Goliath with a bit of a limp and the shirttails of his once crisp uniform hanging out and rumpled.

Some very expensive attempts at image advertising have helped. But a major flaw has been that the campaign sought to change people's perceptions with only the ads and not substantive changes (or justification for the lack of change) regarding those issues that were the subject of controversy about the military.

"The Marines are looking for a few good men" was the theme of an excellent ad campaign that painted the corps as elite, special and proud. The play and film *A Few Good Men* turned the Marine code of honor and obedience into a dishonorable cover for cruelty. Whatever good the ad campaign did to raise the image of the Marine Corps was tarnished by the huge success of the film.

"Be all that you can be" was as strong an ad campaign as any "product" might have had and it wrapped the U.S. Army in a strong image that said "go for it" to a generation that wanted to hear such a message, although it was somewhat unsure about exactly what the *it* in *go for it* was.

Sadly, the pressures of the times, the trends and the sheer numbers have worked against the image of the military services. They are, in the 1990s, just too large and too easy a target for malcontents, social misfits and grandstanding media-savvy lawyers who are good at raising dust for profit and totally unconcerned with the image, care or maintenance of an excellent military machine.

The military services, for their part, have become notoriously good at taking sucker punches. Despite how exciting, new or creative the TV commercials and print ads might be, the military's policies and procedures have changed relatively little over the years. Regulations, codes of honor and discipline that served the military services so well for so long, often seem out-of-date with a society that routinely joins clubs and organizations only to turn around and want the rules changed.

Image advertising is not a complete answer because the budget for a strong, creative campaign, coming as it does from tax dollars, carries a potential for protest. The great gloss on the military's image over the years, at its best moments, resulted in large part from propaganda, a tool that seems ill-suited to the cynical public, special interest groups and media scrutiny that is the order of the day.

If the persons responsible for guiding the military services want to enhance the level of public respect—to regain the image and prestige they had prior to Vietnam—the solution is not likely to be found in slick ads or in the military "reinventing itself" or in employing some of the too-slick and patently transparent PR stunts, such as giving a military action a "name" like "Operation Desert Storm," which plays like a good idea short-term and a bad movie title long-term. Such ersatz efforts at manufactured patriotism tend to prove embarrassing in a historical context. An improved public image may well come from adherence to principles of good marketing. No flashy gimmicks or titles that fit on t-shirts, but a straightforward campaign that could hold up well under scrutiny. The military might consider:

1. *Show the best of what it does well. Often.* The recruiting officers like to promise "career training" so how about testimonials, speeches or profiles on or from men and women who learned the skills that launched successful careers in private life. Or show examples of what peacetime military does in areas of disaster relief or some commendable public service-oriented function.

2. *Dispel myths and misconceptions of what the military is and is not.* People understand the role of the military in war, but what training, assistance or level of preparedness justifies the budget in peacetime?

3. *Tell the public why it should be supportive.* Show the benefits to the consumer, not just a demand for blind, blank-check patriotism.

4. *Bring out the lightning rod.* An articulate spokesperson maintaining a high-profile, answering questions and showing courage and spirit focuses attention—pro and con—in one place, helping to define and reinforce an image. Referring and attributing to departments, committees, secretaries, undersecretaries and attaches only appears to defer responsibility and heighten the

public's disdain for bureaucracy. A single person carrying the torch may stumble occasionally, but at least he or she will not bump into or knock over the other torch carriers and compound confusion.

So this appears naive and simplistic. After all, the military is a part of the Department of Defense with many layers of civilian and military personnel and Congressional committees and sub-committees and things aren't that simple.

Bull.

If there is a person or a committee or a department that has the authority to put tax dollars into ad agency bank accounts for a ". . . few good men" or ". . . all that you can be," then that same entity can implement recommendations such as these.

During a time of public indifference to the military, General Colin Powell and General Arnold Schwartzkopf ranked among the most admired individuals in the United States—perhaps in the world. It would be easy to attribute this to their respective roles in the military action of the Persian Gulf, but it was more than that.

First, it was their high level of visibility. Both men met the press, leaders of government and other public officials on a fairly consistent basis, rising above the image of the faceless military bureaucrats—all pomp and no presence.

Secondly, separately and together, they projected images of intelligence and competence. They were articulate and offered comments of substance. They seemed disciplined, but not wooden. Their public comments suggested strength, yet compassion. Within a year of their names becoming known to the public for the first time, both men were being spoken of as possible presidential candidates. While it's not necessary to go quite that far, the point is the military had in these men not only generals, but symbols of the kind of image the military should hope to project.

At about the same time the two generals were making the U.S. Army look pretty good, the U.S. Navy was figuratively sinking in public opinion. At a social gathering of a ship's crew, outrageous behavior crystallized into what would be called the "Tailhook scandal." An investigation and comments by a number of Navy functionaries—as well as outraged politicians—only served to further confuse the matter in the public's mind. The closest thing to a clean public record of the case is a 1995 made-for-TV movie. The Navy's handling of the matter should be as much an embarrassment as the incident itself.

This was a case where crisis management was called for to maintain public confidence and protect the image of the institution. Doing the right thing was much in order for a variety of reasons.

A major rule of crisis management is to tell your story *first*—and honestly—before your critics announce it for you and define the context of what you'll be called upon to say.

The next rule is to build a reservoir of goodwill from which to draw during bad times. For institutions such as the military services, these goals should actually be in effect at all times, not only in crisis situations.

Talk about what you're doing well.

Create goodwill.

Be honest.

Correct your mistakes. If you don't have the authority to do so, publicly call for such a correction to be done, creating pressure to do so. Sure, this is sometimes breaking ranks, but to do otherwise not only lacks integrity, but starts a potential timebomb ticking as others begin to *demand* that you do something and force you into a defensive posture.

Policies such as these have served the institutions well in the days of their brightest image. Marketing communication firms and agencies demand that clients hold them accountable for efficient management of client budgets. Institutions must do that *at the very least* and an accounting of such efficiencies, when made public, not only quiets critics, but enhances the institution's image.

MARKETING RELIGION

The same social and cultural revolution that both questioned and challenged the sanctity of established institutions hit equally hard at that very epicenter of the community, its churches. Church leaders could say that attendance was down and the size of the average congregation was shrinking in the 1970s because the "new freedoms" sweeping America were in conflict with the restraint and discipline demanded by most religions. Certainly that may have been a large contributing factor, but that overlooks the emergence of a segment of religion that represented a huge growth industry. By the 1980s, many organized religions had never been literally quite so organized, with not only churches, schools, universities and publishing companies in the fold, but television stations, radio stations, hotels and in a couple of cases, even theme parks.

"Televangelists"—a new generation of television ministers—crowded the airwaves and cable channels, flaunting the news of millions of dollars they collected each week from their worldwide "congregations." Many of these ministers, in addition to their pulpits, became frequent figures on the news and talk shows as they led the charge for social and political issues that they described as merely all part of doing the Lord's work. The Reverend Jerry Falwell, one of the more visibly influential ministers, used his TV pulpit to launch "The Moral Majority" and endorsed conservative Republican candidates for public office; Pat Robertson, the host of "The 700 Club," created The Christian Broadcasting Network, later named The Family Channel—a national cable TV powerhouse—and declared his candidacy for the Republican presidential nomination. Reverend Donald Wildmon organized national boycotts and protests against movies and television shows to which he objected.

But then Oral Roberts told his TV audience that the Lord had appeared to him in a dream and "promised to take" him "home" if people did not send in money ($8 million, to be precise) by a specified date; Reverend Jim Bakker was convicted of defrauding the faithful in a time-share condo scam and the Reverend Jimmy Swaggert was photographed with a prostitute at a cheap motel. A seemingly large number of Catholic priests were implicated in scandals involving sex. All in all, it was a pretty bad time for organized religion, the churches and those people charged with the responsibility for keeping them open. The image of churches and preachers was as low as the spirits of the disenchanted parishioners and congregations that had put their faith in them. They were feeling let down. Clearly, it would be inappropriate to assign blame for this situation and these occurrences to the social and cultural revolution.

By the dawn of the 1990s, to say that America's churches had an image problem was an understatement. As rich, prominent, influential and visible as many of the "televangelists" were, polls continued to show that the most trusted man in America was former CBS News anchorman, Walter Cronkite, who had stepped down from that post in 1981.

Obviously, many dedicated members of the clergy were doing their best to serve the needs of their congregations in the face of the excesses of their more conspicuous brethren. Yet, church attendance was down, cynicism was up and the public seemed to be building a disdain for clergymen with computerized mailing lists. Circumstances might have favored subtlety in promotional matters in church circles.

The New York Times published a series titled "Mega-churches." One headline read, "Religion Goes to Market to Expand Congregation." The article told of a community church in South Barrington, Illinois, that draws more than 15,000 people a week. A poster hanging outside the pastor's office reads, "What is our business? Who is our customer? What does the customer value?"

Those words of management guru Peter F. Drucker are not exactly the typical addendum to the Ten Commandments. The minister of the church had served previously in a church in California which was known for its slogan "Where the Flock Likes to Rock." This time the minister was reported to be designing a new church service intended to increase attendance at service even more—one, he said, which would "have elements of 'Letterman' in that it will be unpredictable."

Such unpredictability is affordable, it appears, thanks to the church's (1995) budget of $12.35 million, about 63 percent of which pays for 260 full-time and part-time employees. That would be the minister, the organist, the custodian and 257 others. The balance went to "operating expenses" and the mortgage on the church's $34.3 million building.

This is not to be critical of commerce and industry or to look askance at a thriving local enterprise that employs 260 people. The fact that the enterprise is a church in a suburb of Chicago might yield a clue to people's growing cynicism about institutions in general and why, increasingly, churches are so concerned about their images. In a sense, it might be viewed as commendable that a church was employing modern marketing techniques to build attendance and interest. So did Reverend Bakker before he was sent to prison.

As images go, among churches and religious figures, few would argue that Mother Theresa is perhaps the closest person to a living 20th-century saint anyone is likely to find. And her digs didn't cost $34.3 million. The magic marketing formula she stumbled upon was to spread religion as it was intended to be—with charity and love and without snappy one-liners and acting like a stand-up comic as a means to draw a crowd on Sunday mornings. Of course, it is odd to tell a church—or any other business with the kind of numbers the church in the example posts—that they are doing anything wrong. The numbers look great, especially the 15,000 people per week. It suggests they are giving the public what it wants.

For now.

The movie "Die Hard 3" packed theaters for a while as well. It made a fortune by what many people would say was giving the public a large dose of what it wanted. Yet, down the street, critics complained about the sad state of the film industry.

The clergy have always known it wasn't just the fire-and-brimstone sermons that kept people coming back, it was in no small part the interesting and *entertaining* experience of church-going. But where does one draw the line and when?

There will always be some very full and thriving churches. And clergymen will be asking what it will take to bring people in and it will take, to a degree, a marketing plan with objectives, strategy and tactics. But the empty suffering churches will look at the wealthy thriving churches and in part criticize their lack of honesty in addressing Mr. Drucker's third question: What does the customer value?

When it comes to a church, they may suggest, the correct answer should not be that it is an entertaining and unpredictable experience that reminds them of the "David Letterman Show." It should suggest something about hope, peace, love, comfort, guidance, and spirituality, and charity. A $34 million building, while very likely a magnificent structure, says little about the values that a church should represent in its community.

As stories of fraud, deceit and sexual misconduct cause people to reconsider their involvement with churches, and more churches and religious denominations lament the tarnishing of their image, it is appropriate to ask, in Peter Drucker's words, "What is our business and who are our customers?" But, more than the questioning, it is the *answers* that will define the image. If the church's answer is that it stands for *giving* and *helping* in the community, rather than merely entertaining, the image of that church and by example, other churches will be enhanced. If the answers include putting resources into the community and programs for the congregation with a dollar figure that is proportionally more significant than what goes toward the mortgage of a $34.3 million building, then a church's image will be enhanced.

Few churches have buildings, budgets, and congregations comparable in size to that used in the example, but everything is relative. The expenses and politics of a church—as in any other "business"—will not go away, nor likely diminish. But its sense of purpose will be reflected in its image in its community. And its purpose should be its priority if it is to win the loyalty and support of its constituents. If any institution should, if for no other reason than as part of its marketing plan, "lead by example" in terms of modern day imagery, it is the church. It is also part of the tradition of churches that those who do good do well. Offering and publicizing day care programs, self-help programs, counseling, tutoring, seniors assistance and such breed loyalty and commitment in the community.

True, some particular churches may be known to "pack 'em in" with entertaining services and programs, but "The Beverly Hillbillies," "Three's Company," and "Dynasty" were all number one for a while too. And when people eventually came to find them not-so-entertaining, they folded. Flash is flash and rarely, if ever, makes it for the long haul.

MARKETING HIGHER EDUCATION

Among other institutions fairly regarded as being bigger than a breadbox (and frequently under fire) are colleges and universities. The starting point for learning, character-building, practicing one's social skills and building wonderful memories, institutions of higher learning have almost throughout history been short on funding and prominent in controversy. Predictably then, their images have shifted from one of "setting the standards" to offering accommodation in instance after instance from sports programs recruiting, to course planning, to "political correctness."

In his best-selling book *Culture of Complaint,* Robert Hughes notes, "Major American universities are big business, disposing of immense investments in stock and real estate, plugged into government by countless advisory pipelines. . . . Much of the traditional teaching in American schools, though not necessarily the machine of thought-bending its critics now claim it was, has been rather less 'disinterested' than it seems." Mr. Hughes goes on to quote historian Eugene Genovese as saying, "We have transformed our colleges from places of higher learning into places for the technical training of poorly prepared young men and women who need a degree to get a job in a college-crazy society."

The world may indeed be crazy—college and otherwise—but the problems of college and university images are not all that unique, nor are they irreversible.

Political conservatives charge colleges are typically a hotbed of liberalism. Liberals don't necessarily argue the point, but add that the places all seem to be run by moneyed conservatives who, while often not teaching, run the boards, *hire* the teachers and handle the cash. The 1990s saw smaller colleges running ads that looked a lot like the ads summer camps used to run several decades earlier. Well-scrubbed girls, with hair pulled back, sat contemplating a pond or tree. Young men, still sporting "preppy" attire, seemed to be looking for the tennis courts. The suggestion might be that college life hadn't changed much since 1949.

The images of specific colleges and universities have remained fairly consistent over the years by deliberately keeping a low profile while maintaining high academic standards and avoiding scandals. Cheating scandals, rigging and tampering with quota admissions, filtering gifts or cash to athletes to become "students" all cast a negative shadow over colleges and universities in general. One school's bad apple being caught often creates the impression with the public that a particular practice is widespread and that others merely haven't been caught . . . yet. Just as one malpracticing professional can leave a taint on an entire profession, so does a school with problems leave people wondering how widespread a problem might be "industry-wide."

Too often, grandstanding politicians have painted colleges with a broad brush. A demonstration or incident on a single campus will trigger comments about the decline of order "on our college campuses." An absurd theory offered by a single professor will inspire remarks about the quality of information "on our college campuses" and suddenly all schools are on the defensive.

This is another example of a need for basic crisis management: When the media or the public is criticizing slackers in your industry, how do you manage to distance yourself from the negative perceptions—and realities—while still maintaining a pride in the industry or profession itself?

Individual schools should have their own marketing plans just as they have operating plans and fundraising plans. And *image* should be a factor in marketing plans. The ad campaign that uses the theme line "A Mind Is a Terrible Thing to Waste" for the United Negro College Fund is every bit as powerful in its imagery as the U.S. Army's "Be all that you can be." But great ad themes and headlines should represent something substantive *behind* the headlines.

Schools individually need to create their images based on their individual uniqueness: the business school, the art school, the drama school or the technology school.

This is an area where buzzwords help. A technical school that calls itself an "institute" helps define the image to which it aspires. A drama "workshop" or "performing arts center" suggests a grander image than simply "school" or "college" suggests.

Beyond "name brand" distinctions, frequent newsletters and on-site seminars and workshops display signs of life and vitality. Too often the alumni are hit-up in several fundraising campaigns per year and perhaps an annual dinner or weekend. Ongoing participation in as many forms as possible creates the reservoir of goodwill as well as energy and momentum that invite community support.

Collectively, schools need to counter the image that any one controversy is reflective of every college and university. Again, symposia, roundtables and joint projects provide image enhancement.

When the securities exchanges and the commodities futures exchanges in Chicago recognized that their own intense rivalry (and occasional sniping at one another) was hurting all of them and causing business to be directed to their New York competitors, they decided collectively to lower their voices. They also produced a magazine that was inserted into the Sunday *Chicago Tribune.* Titled *The Chicago Exchanges,* it reviewed with great pride the public, commercial and professional benefits the five exchanges brought to the city and the world financial community. The resulting goodwill and the extended "shelf-life" use of this piece as a public relations vehicle was worth hundreds of times its modest production and media cost.

A similar principle, with some adaptation, would serve institutions of higher education well. All of the colleges in the United States are not likely to speak with one voice, nor do they need to. There are certainly enough professional associations to enable a series of publications or programs to be generated that will emphasize on a consistent, ongoing basis what is right about colleges today. To mount a modest effort by which representatives of higher education speak with one voice should be easily managed. Of course, there will be competition for funding, grants, endowments and the incoming contingent of the best and brightest among both students and faculty. But it is counterproductive to do nothing or to isolate themselves from one another, the profession and the community and to concede the determination of how and what people think of them in the future to those radicals, mavericks and opportunists who may not nearly reflect their attitudes and conditions. To create and roll out a program represents a great deal more in potential gains than losses. To simply go about pursuing one's own agenda without concern for the larger context invites someone else to define future rules of order.

MARKETING THE CITY, THE STATE OR THE COUNTRY

You've heard about it, read about it, talked about it . . . now stay away from it.

Increasingly, the media's been trumpeting the bad news, and it doesn't matter how good what you've got may be if the public is afraid to come and check it out.

Florida depends mightily on tourism, meetings and conventions for its economic survival. A series of tourist murders, hurricanes and floods seemed to suddenly change the sunshine state into a disaster area. Between rising violent crime and natural disasters, no meeting planner or travel agent could take responsibility for a Florida booking.

The highly publicized violent crime in both Washington, D.C. and Detroit (tied for the distinction of "murder capital of America") made these cities travellers would want to bypass.

Chicago has been trying to disassociate itself from Al Capone and "the mob" for more than 50 years.

Just the mention of certain places in a television monologue— Cleveland, Kansas, New Jersey—was a sure bet to draw laughs from the audience.

Internationally? The French are rude; people are being shot on the beaches in Jamaica; and Mexico is all right unless you drink the water or encounter a policeman.

Such images are enough to make people stay home and do nothing—two situations that historically are not good for business.

The concept and practice of image marketing is ideally suited to such eclectic entities as cities, states and countries. The Chambers of Commerce and Economic Development Commissions have been showing their slide presentations and passing around brochures for generations. Obviously, whether the subject location is work, home, or play, the factors of security, accessibility, convenience, climate and taxes are normally matters outside the control of marketers. Yet the perception of value to the target audience *is* the marketer's role.

Too often, entities that have never advertised before believe that coming up with a print ad or a TV spot that shows smiling models over happy music, while an announcer proclaims, "This is a great place to live and work" is all it takes.

Alas, we're not convinced.

The town or state (or country) that gets excited over the fact that it's finally advertising runs the risk of creating "preaching to the choir"–type of advertising.

So they have nice weather, sandy beaches and happy people. So do hundreds of locations.

In 1995, Los Angeles County chose for itself a new slogan: "Together, We're the Best. Los Angeles." It was to be the centerpiece of a five-year $5 million campaign.

The New York Times reported this selection of the line under a heading that declared "New slogan for L.A. accentuates pride but lacks pizzazz." The paper was being extremely charitable in its observation. The line, quite simply, is *awful*. It gives no information, no benefit or value and is, to say the least, subject to some debate.

Rejected suggestions reportedly included, "You Can Shake Us, But You Can't Break Us," "Diversity Is the Key, Los Angeles the Place to Be" and "Los Angeles is No. 1, One for All and All for One."

Apparently 1995 was also a year for a drought in good slogan ideas for the southern California area.

First, it doesn't *need* a *slogan* at all. People don't move, visit or invest because of slogans. Second, if you're going to invite people to come to you, give them a *reason*. "Together, We're the Best . . ." not only doesn't specify "the best of *what*," but it doesn't provide a compelling (or even vaguely interesting) reason to go to Los Angeles. For years, the city had been associated with sunshine, movie stars, glamor and warm temperatures. It was also known for crime, smog, crowded freeways, bad public transportation and an unaffordable standard of living.

How about offering a tax incentive to businesses that move to L.A.? Or tuition subsidies to employees of new or relocated companies to help achieve a better educated population.

How about giving vacationers a coupon book for free or discounted services or admissions? Again, people respond to promotions that benefit *them,* not the advertisers, first.

Slogans, presumably intended to encourage local pride, belong on license plates and public buildings. A $5 million campaign to put a shine on a tarnished image must give something to the people it's seeking to reach: a free concert in the park or at a mall, a widely promoted (and covered) meal to needy families or a beach clean-up are *feel good* promotions that will be talked about and remembered for what they say about the priorities of the sponsor.

A few years earlier, pre-slogan Los Angeles had a contest to choose a new *song* for its city. While the effort didn't make much of an impression over time (as had the song), conceptually the idea was better placed. A song is an "involving" thing that people can share and the pride—as well as the *prize*—was a more upbeat attempt at image enhancement. Like school songs or any other well-worked theme music, city or state songs help a great deal to promote a mental picture or a mood. Consider some songs, anthems, pop and rock and roll, that have helped both directly and indirectly to promote a city or state. Even a country weeper about love or hearts left behind serves to remind people of places where memories are made . . .

The list in Exhibit 7.1 is the lighter side of image marketing. The introduction of a song at a summer music festival is a way to get attention and share perceptions while giving people something they can take away and *share*. Unlike a slogan, it can be a place's gift to its people and its visitors.

Image campaigns for cities and states are rich in opportunities for powerful advertising and PR:

- Touting the number and quality of schools as opportunities for learning.
- Touting the number and quality of parks, lakes, rivers, museums, galleries, amusement attractions and free things to do on weekends.
- Promoting favorable cost of living/quality of life to that of comparable cities or states.
- Promoting your area as a center of artistic or technical advancement by having an (at least) annual film festival, food festival, art festival, concert series, theater seasons,

Abilene
Allentown
Amarillo
Big Noise from Winnetka
Blue Moon of Kentucky
Bowling Green
By the Time I Get to
  Phoenix
California Dreamin'
California Girls
California, Here I Come
California Sun
Carolina on My Mind
Chattanooga Choo-Choo
Chicago
Detroit City
Do You Know the Way to
  San Jose?
Do You Know What It
  Means to Miss New
  Orleans?
Galveston
Gary, Indiana
Georgia on My Mind
Hollywood Nights
Houston
I Left My Heart in San
  Francisco
Jackson
Kentucky Means Paradise

Kentucky Rain
Kentucky Woman
L.A., You're My Lady
Louisiana Man
Memphis
Midnight Train to Georgia
Moonlight in Vermont
Nashville Cats
New Orleans
New York State of Mind
Please Come to Boston
St. Louis Blues
San Antonio Rose
San Francisco Bay Blues
San Francisco—Wear
  Some Flowers in Your
  Hair
Seattle
Stars Fell on Alabama
Starwood in Aspen
Sweet Home Alabama
Tallahassee Lassie
Texas in My Rear-View
  Mirror
The Lady Came from
  Baltimore
Tupelo Honey
Walkin' to New Orleans
Washington Square
Weekend in New England

EXHIBIT 7.1

50 Familiar Songs that Call Attention to a Place

etc. Of course, none of these ideas are especially new or creative, but the fact is, they all work. Just because an idea is a formula approach that people have shown they enjoy, doesn't mean it should automatically be dismissed in favor of moving on to something new. People complain that (like ads themselves) there are too many festivals and award ceremonies. Yet, crowds keep coming back again to support such activities.

- Offering radio stations and newspapers in other cities all expense paid trips to *your* city is another way to cost effectively advance the image of your city as a desirable place to be.

Local tourism bureaus can still create TV commercials and print ads with attractive women in bathing suits, and beautiful, happy couples smiling, holding hands and dancing; ads showing everyone what a great time is to be had in the magical place of dreams that is paying for the commercial. But as more and more resorts, cruise lines, cities and countries have run those spots, they have become generic. Images are built around an identification with an event, a site or a benefit that cannot be enjoyed in a thousand other places.

The promotional ideas and the attractions themselves are as available as the imaginative minds in your marketing department or agency. But when the big blockbuster idea doesn't materialize immediately, don't be resistant to the formula approaches. They've become formulaic for good reasons.

The most important point to remember is to be *visible*—to be out front showing a presence. And to know that, just as the most effective product advertising succeeds because it gives the market prospect a *reason to buy,* image marketing may have a different, long-term goal. The rules, however, are the same: give your constituent group a reason to like you, to want to support you and to refer others your way.

Slogans, particularly slogans like "We're the best," are not a good reason.

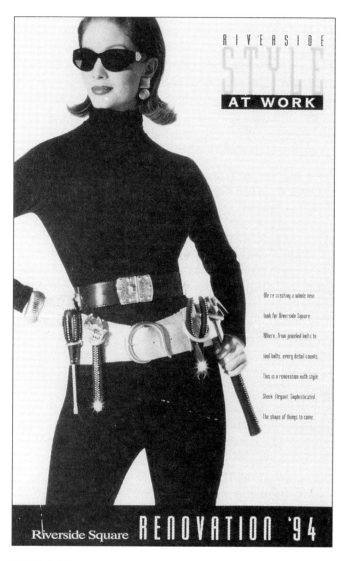

EXHIBIT 7.2

Riverside Square (1)

Riverside Square, once a dark '70s-style New Jersey Mall, underwent a major renovation that included oriental rugs, designer seating and fresh flower arrangements. Following the theme "Unlike Any Other Shopping Center," the operative word was *style,* symbolized by the "catsuit lady"—an upscale fashion figure that appeared in ads, on-site displays and even on the barricades used during the renovation.

RIVERSIDE SQUARE Presents

Decorating With Antiques
A Show And Sale
Wednesday, January 12 - Saturday, January 15

More than 30 antique dealers from throughout the Northeast, featuring Early American,
Art Deco and Victorian furniture. Suites entirely decorated in period pieces.
A showcase of quilts, fine china, prints and collectibles.
Plus crystal and glass repair on the First Level
near the main escalator.

Riverside Square ◆

Bloomingdale's, Saks Fifth Avenue, Conran's Habitat and 80 other fine stores and restaurants
Monday through Friday, 10:00 a.m. to 9:30 p.m. Saturday, 10:00 a.m. to 7:00 p.m.
Route 4 (Hackensack Avenue North Exit) between the GW Bridge and Garden State Parkway, Hackensack, New Jersey. 201/489-0151.

EXHIBIT 7.3

Riverside Square (2)
Exhibits and displays rich in imagery, such as the warm, nostalgic show
"Decorating with Antiques," helped to attract crowds to Riverside Square after its
renovation.

EXHIBIT 7.4

Merchandise Mart (Chicago)

Shopping malls are typically characterized by their stores and shops, whether unique specialty stores or major chain store "anchors." To distinguish themselves from other shopping areas, malls or centers might showcase an event or exhibit that reflects an image they wish their market would associate with them. Chicago's Merchandise Mart's Shopping area "The Shops at the Mart" hoped the *Warhol Exhibition Limited Tour* would reflect the facility's own artistic imagery and style and set it apart.

MARKETING DOCTORS, LAWYERS AND POLITICAL FIGURES

Some of the most prestigious professions in modern American life are having major image problems in the 1990s and they are turning to advertising and public relations for help. Some of the best agencies are using TV to try to fix the problem, which is ironic because television is in no small part the reason the problem exists.

Images of doctors and the medical profession derive perhaps 10 percent from personal experience and 90 percent from what is represented in movies and on TV. People know a lot of what they think they know about doctors from their close-up observation of the profession over time on "Dr. Kildare," "Ben Casey," "Marcus Welby, M.D.," "Dr. Christian," "Medical Center," "M*A*S*H," and "E.R." Medical personnel work all day and all night, become intimately involved in patients' personal lives and never deny services to people who can't pay. That was the image.

Then "60 Minutes" began telling people how much hospitals actually charged for aspirin. The rougher tabloid TV shows showed the worst horror stories of error and neglect. One story even had a doctor delay the release of critical information about the AIDS virus until his own work on the subject could be considered for a Nobel Prize. Investigative reports developed statistics on alcoholism and drug addiction among doctors. But things got worse.

America's two most prestigious professions, doctors and lawyers, discovered each other, and malpractice suits proliferated. And, as the amount of the judgments and settlements grew, so proportionately did the amount of media coverage—and the cost of malpractice insurance—until the spiral had soared into orbit. As is the case with spirals, doctors' fees went up to cover insurance, tests administered went up to protect the doctors and patients' impatience with the matter became public.

People got mad at their doctors. Doctors complained that patients brought it on themselves with frivolous and unjustified malpractice suits. Insurance companies took the high road and insisted that doctors, lawyers and patients were all equally to blame and that, in any event, *they* weren't paying.

A Chicago ophthalmologist was publicly criticized by both the media and his profession for opening a chain of eye care and surgical centers and using advertising and telemarketing to get more patients. The least of the slurs against him was that he had turned surgeries into an assembly line process and was using the operating room as his factory.

The New York Times reported that one doctor sued another, claiming the second doctor was performing surgeries with *his* patented technique. The first doctor demanded that the second doctor "and any other surgeon brandishing a knife the same way must pay him a royalty." The same article noted "many entrepreneurial doctors are now winning patents on commonly used methods of practicing medicine. . . ."

The Chairman of the American Medical Association's Council on Judicial and Ethical Affairs called the practice "wrong," adding that his A.M.A. Council had decided that patenting of such procedures "violated the Hippocratic oath as well as the A.M.A.'s guiding ethics" on the matter. Another doctor countered: "The Hippocratic oath says nothing about intellectual property." A member of Congress offered that such practice will "increase the cost of health care and limit access of patients and other doctors to new techniques."

Many more instances and anecdotes can be offered, but the point is pretty clear: The image of the doctor as a dedicated healer whose main purpose in his or her professional life is to keep people alive, first and foremost, is fading. Worse, the image that is replacing it is one of an insensitive, indifferent opportunist, profiteer and angler.

Still worse is that, to a large degree, the doctors have brought this on themselves. Lawyers had a major hand in it and the greedy individuals who sought to cash-in big by exploiting the malpractice issue can't be dismissed.

Greedy or enterprising?

Who cares?

Placing blame is not the issue, since there seems to be quite enough to go around. The baby boomers who grew up to be "the Me Generation" and doctors had no great passion to become "Dr. Kildare," but to combine all they had learned in business and technology. While no one ever suggested that the many fictional role models were poor, they were never represented as flaunting their success. Modern doctors asked, "What's wrong with saving lives *and* being rich?"

Technically and legally, nothing.

But if concerns settled only on matters of the technical and legal, a word like *image* may not even exist. It is not enough anymore to be regarded as a brilliant and skillful doctor. You must also display sensitivity and a bit of humility or the list of those who wish you ill will keep growing until one day, the story goes, it will wrap itself around you. Legends have grown of investment bankers, real estate developers, hotel owners, media moguls, lawyers and, alas, doctors whose arrogance and egos have caused cheers to go up as they fell from great heights.

Why risk it?

If image affects your business—and it does—build a practice and market your services with an image that enhances your reputation, wins supporters and respect and alienates the fewest number of people.

Going back to the basic elements of the marketing plan (situation analysis, objectives, strategy and tactics), define who and what you want to be. More than one objective is okay, as long as one is *primary* and the others are secondary or subordinated. Doctors can indeed be doctors, investors, moguls, authors, teachers, lecturers, association officers, lobbyists, publishers, fundraisers, missionaries and hosts of radio call-in shows.

But which of these is to be the *day job* and which, in order of priority, comes after, knowing that few of us have the capacity—much less the time—to be truly outstanding at more than one thing at a time?

Doctors who concentrate on being outstanding doctors and let others handle their investments, business interests and publicity, make fewer enemies and even earn greater respect and, most likely, referrals. The doctor who sought to patent the surgical technique by simply selling (or having his business agent sell) the technique to a medical research or practice facility, could have let the business people argue the propriety and legal issues, while maintaining the integrity of his profession and his practice and avoiding the disdain of the AMA, his colleagues and perhaps his patients as well.

154

It's all about people.

You learn, then pass it on to others. Whether it's fishing, or more important things. Like caring. And concern. It's what Leif Erickson, Sr., M.D. taught his son Leif Erickson, Jr. M. D. And, as a part of Aurora, what they both give back to the community.

Drs. Leif Erickson Sr. and Sr. Burlington Wisconsin

AuroraHealthCare

EXHIBIT 7.5

Aurora Health Care

At a time when the public's respect for doctors and the health care community in general is declining, Wisconsin's Aurora Health Care puts the focus on people in a campaign that is touching and powerful in its imagery of two generations of doctors reflecting the values of their community.

"Isn't that unfair?," a five-year-old might ask. "Can't he do both?"

Yes, he can. But if his profession and his patients see his entrepreneurial spirit as greed, his practice will suffer. Doctors can't go from being comfortable (or even wealthy) to fabulously wealthy without making certain compromises along the way that will alienate some people—a few of whom may be quite vocal on the subject.

This is true of any profession. But doctors are held to higher standards in part because they seek such respect and distinction. The safest way to have the image and recognition you may be seeking is to follow some classic medical advice and pursue it by practicing *moderation.*

Let others write *about* you, as opposed to seeking major author status. The successful medical professionals in this category quickly become celebrity authors first with their roles as *doctors* ultimately (and quickly) being subordinated.

Let architects, fundraisers and builders build the clinic with your name on it and let other doctors refer patients to you because you are competent, fair and ethical—not because you own the clinic. It is another example of operating in an environment of *doing well by doing good.*

The approach may be simplistic, but it works. Donating services to a free clinic or homeless shelter, pledging a percentage of your income to a scholarship fund for future doctors, returning calls and being available to sustain the image the public has and *wants to have* of doctors—such basics still translate to business.

Hippocrates directed that doctors, "First do no harm." The phrase carried a mantle of nobility, and one could certainly do worse than to have nobility as part of his or her image.

The bashing doctors have taken in modern times is mild compared to that of lawyers. Bookstores have entire sections now devoted to volumes on lawyer jokes, which have replaced mother-in-law jokes, dumb blonde jokes and ethnic jokes in contemporary cocktail party conversations. The Christmas 1994 season featured some 10 major studio releases centered around lawyers—mostly portraying them as devious, unprincipled, greedy and manipulative.

Whew!

The lawyers' typical reaction? They cry "foul." The profession that has tried to explain to us that life is often unfair, has now claimed it was being slandered and represented unfairly.

And does a day pass without someone quoting Shakespeare's famous "First, we kill all the lawyers" line? Let's not try to analyze the significance, if any, in Queen Elizabeth hosting a banquet for the American Bar Association and serving hot dogs. That was 1957 and it's fair to suggest things have only gotten worse since then.

It seemed clear that the image of lawyers was in real trouble when the attackers numbered among them . . . lawyers!

No stranger to criticism and ridicule, then-Vice President of the United States, Dan Quayle, himself a lawyer (as was his wife), attacked lawyers, claiming there were too many of them, their fees were too high and that their actions drove up costs for everyone. Curiously, this is the same argument people usually advance about TV commercials. At any rate, spokesmen for state bar associations, predictably and unconvincingly, responded to Mr. Quayle, noting the contributions lawyers make to society and how the American system could not function without them. As a truth, this offered small comfort in that critics charged that it was lawyers who *built* the system in such a way as to *assure* that it could not function without them.

In the midst of a debate, two sad notes were sounded: first, a lawyer was shot to death by the husband of his client and, second, a Bar Association spokesperson blamed the incident on the proliferation of "lawyer jokes" which he claimed were fueling people's hatred of lawyers and he demanded that the jokes stop. The situation seemed to run from obscene to absurd.

The American Bar Association itself is not short of trouble, image or otherwise. The organization, with a staff of some 750 and a 1995 budget of $118 million, has long been regarded as a group representing rich and powerful lawyers at large and powerful firms. Its accrediting system for law schools has been under investigation by the U.S. Department of Justice. In addition, it has come under fire from deans of prestigious law schools and has been the subject of a massive antitrust lawsuit. A *Chicago Tribune* story noted that the Massachusetts School of Law charged the ABA accrediting group with being a "cartel" that "controls salaries, employment conditions and tuition." More than a year after the suit was filed, the ABA's own legal bills totaled more than $1 million and the case hadn't yet gone to trial.

In addition, after the association took a public position in support of abortion rights and handgun control, several thousand ABA members resigned.

How the formerly exaulted legal profession fell into nearly as much disrepute as the clients whose offensive conduct lawyers are called upon to defend comes down to two main causes: ego and (no surprise) money.

The lawyer's role models—the people who personified what lawyers wanted to be—were men such as Clarence Darrow or Oliver Wendell Holmes or the fictional superlawyer, Perry Mason. Modern-day high-profile lawyers such as F. Lee Bailey, William Kunstler and Alan Dershowitz appear more concerned about their own celebrity status as authors and television talk show guests. When they *do* practice law, it appears they only do so under TV lights and for weighty fees that reach seven-figures. Their egos are likely to weigh in at a similar weight.

The profession's image was not enhanced by a 1995 *New York Times* story on lawyer's fees:

- A suit against six major airlines charged with price-fixing of fares resulted in the plaintiffs in the action receiving airline future travel coupons with a total of between $8 and $25 million. Legal fees were more than $14 million.

- A suit against General Motors that charged possible safety problems on certain GM-manufactured trucks netted 6.4 million people about $1,000 each in future truck purchase discounts. The lawyers' bills were $19 million.

- Intel's Pentium computer chip was said to be causing calculation errors. A suit against the company resulted in customers pretty much getting a replacement chip. The lawyers' bills were $6 million.

Separately, a full-page ad appeared numerous times in major newspapers. It was signed by nine professional trade associations under the headline, "The Lawyers said they'd take care of everything, but they only took care of themselves." The ad notes suits filed by lawyers on behalf of investors. Without the suits ever going to trial, one was settled and a participating investor received $250, while the lawyer received $3.3 million. In a second suit, the same investor received $441 and the lawyers $7.5 million.

These cases may not be "typical," but the image damage to lawyers occurs when such cases are deemed "reflective" of what the profession has become.

Ethics and morality suggest a lawyer's fee for services should not exceed the amount of compensation received by his or her client. Too many lawyers, however, do not agree. They insist they work hard, put in a lot of time and earn their fees. But, as *The New York Times* article notes, "While lawyers may reap small fortunes, the cases are sometimes quickly resolved without witnesses being deposed. In a case with Chrysler involving defective heater coils . . . lawyers for both sides hammered out a settlement proposal after about 20 hours of face-to-face meetings. . . . Plaintiffs' lawyers' fees and expenses in that case came to $1.65 million."

A bad tendency among lawyers is to want to call a press conference as they leave court or a settlement meeting, to brag about the huge award they've just arranged or to cry foul if a decision goes against them. Big judgments are viewed as vehicles for exploitation to generate more business. Losses are viewed as new opportunities to file petitions for reconsideration or appeals . . . and bill more time.

Lawyers doing pro bono or reduced fee-work for those who can't afford help are being grossly upstaged and overshadowed on a daily basis by the media hungry, flashy egomaniacs and opportunists of the profession. The situation is very similar to that facing doctors, where the "grandstanders" create an impression that they are typical of their profession.

The trial of sports figure O.J. Simpson has been called by the media "The Trial of the Century." We should hope not. The media, of course, has its job to do, and "The Trial of the Century" is likely to generate better ratings than "Another L.A. Murder Trial."

But by showing the lengths to which some lawyers will go to avoid the truth coming out—while passionately insisting they want *only* the truth—the image of the legal system suffers. *Badly.* The clear impression the public receives is of arrogance, ego and lack of integrity that will drive people to say anything or do anything to win a decision whether justice is served or not.

Worse yet, major media covering the trial hired dozens of lawyers as consultants who, while each preened in their on-camera spotlights, educated the public in ways that were clearly not intended. Rather than presenting valuable information on applicable rules of law, one by one they sought to show the audience how smart *they* were by proposing ideas the other lawyers should have used to avoid having the truth come out, thus swaying the public's and the jury's emotions.

It's great entertainment, but is it justice? The profession's image of lawyers must be to work tirelessly to see that their clients receive fairness and justice, not a pass on a technicality.

How do lawyers concerned about their tarnished image fight back and regain the prestige and dignity they appear to have lost?

Remember the only way a marketing plan's elements can be effective is if they are drawn honestly. That means the situation analysis must accurately reflect the situation and not what you'd like to "interpret" the situation to be. People often apply the phrase "They just don't get it" to lawyers who insist on answering critics with a dismissive suggestion that the critics just don't understand that critics' views have no value.

Once you clearly understand the situation, set your objectives and devise your strategy and tactics. The way to insure that the "grandstanders" are not accepted as reflective of the profession is to tell people so. When a William Kunstler, Alan Dershowitz or F. Lee Bailey stresses the importance of "using the media" to win, they actually mean *manipulating* the media. Their efforts to do so are transparent to apparently everyone but themselves and are contributing factors to people's sense that lawyers whom people have trusted with their lives, cannot be trusted. It doesn't help when the high-profile showmen of the profession dismiss their record of losses by simple references to jealous rivals trying to embarrass them. These folks who've helped to tarnish the image of their profession do not embarrass easily.

Show some humility. People are angry with lawyers and doctors because (in addition to high fees) they think the members of the profession don't care. Show that you do. Making money is great; being confident is great; being successful is great; being a jerk is not great. As a wise person once suggested: try checking your ego at the door.

Listen. A common complaint directed at lawyers is that they so often, after the first meeting, seem to be distracted, inattentive or preoccupied with something else. The client is your customer. He or she is paying your bill and deserves your attention.

Be courteous. This isn't boy scout stuff—it's real. A frequent complaint is that lawyers are slow to return phone calls or don't answer questions and give the impression that the client is a pest for asking. If you're too busy to call back, have an associate or an assistant do it.

Charge fairly. This, too, may seem simplistic, yet the trend since at least the 1980s is to suggest that because you charge more, you're better. This is nonsense. Lawyers such as those in the Chrysler example who bill $1.65 million for 20 hours plus of, presumably, preparation time, should have a hard time not laughing at their own absurdity in thinking their time is really worth upwards of $80,000 per hour. People who believe they were charged fairly don't complain, they call again, refer business and speak well and often of you.

Devote a portion of each week to pro bono work. Many lawyers and firms say they do this, but in fact it is the younger, inexperienced beginners or the lowest ranking employees of the firm who actually do. It is an investment in yourself and your community and it helps create the sort of image that breeds admiration . . . and more business. A charge frequently hurled at lawyers is that they profit from the misery of others. No fees for a certain number of hours each week can help to negate that criticism while projecting a positive image.

Guarantee your work. After you've had a moment to recover from the shock, note that the suggestion is not to guarantee the *outcome,* but just the quality of service—something that for years has been a "given" in most businesses. A Chicago law firm began offering clients a written service guarantee and told the *Chicago Tribune,* "We have years of research that shows that service is the single most important issue to clients." Noting that clients are becoming more demanding and law firms more competitive, the agreements provide cost adjustments and refunds for the dissatisfied.

Your image marketing plan might also include doing (or having a public relations person or agency do) a newsletter in which you comment—in plain English—on legal matters in the news to an audience of past and present clients and the *media*. It is an excellent image-building, referral-prospecting, and goodwill-creating device: controlled and cost effective.

Finally, in addition to the previously mentioned pro bono work, offer your services (free if necessary) to a good cause in your community. Good lawyers immediately respond by saying they don't have the time to spare and, besides, they've got bills to pay, too. Consider this an investment in practice development to donate your services to a shelter, church, rehab center or home for the aged in your community, as a way of building a reservoir of goodwill. It is the sort of move that causes people to react to the next lawyer-bashing joke they hear or the latest media grandstanding by a legal egomaniac with a simple, "Well, they're not *all* like that."

On the subject of being "tarred with the same brush," politicians as a group have never been held in especially high regard. It is interesting then to note surveys that show their public esteem continually going ever *lower*.

To marketers, those charged with checking the pulse and mood of the country and finding the "products" it wants or perceives it needs, there is a certain irony in noting the progressive lessening of respect, admiration and appreciation by the public at large for those in whom it invests the control of its legal, social, economic and political environment.

Of course, a case can be made that the same situation has been in effect throughout history, that a certain disdain and resentment for the ruler (and the ruling class) isn't new. There are those who say that to question authority isn't necessarily bad. And there are those who are suspicious of anyone who would want a greater degree of power or control than his or her neighbors have. Yet, for all that, we still make our judgments about those in whom we entrust power based upon their images.

Since the Watergate scandal and the resignation of President Nixon, the public and the media have not felt obliged, it seems, to show much in the way of good manners towards candidates and elected officials. In fairness, few elected officials have done much to positively distinguish themselves, preferring to speak in "sound bites" that, while appearing forceful and decisive, don't say anything:

We can do more and we must do more.

We must move forward.

I can make a difference.

I share your concern.

I feel passionately about that.

People deserve an opportunity.

There are no easy answers.

I stand for change.

I am a different kind of candidate.

I promise a new beginning.

In politics, image is everything. Candidate George Bush, in an attempt to make a specific, hard-hitting statement, thundered, "Read my lips—no new taxes." The line came back to haunt him when he subsequently signed a new tax bill. It was not only his political enemies, but many of his friends who spoke against him. He had taken on the image of a man who, while perhaps well-intentioned, could not be believed.

John F. Kennedy set the standard with his election in 1960. Until then, it was rare to hear the word "charisma" applied to an American politician. After his election, politics, campaigns and candidates become more conscious than ever before in history, on such matters as style, tone, appearance and image.

After decades of elderly, partly bald—even rumpled—candidates and officeholders, Mr. Kennedy's image of youth, vigor, wit, charm, grace—and hair—became the model for future candidates, whether the office was President of the United States or Chairman of the local museum board. Future candidates who presented images of charm, wit, youth, etc., were described as "Kennedyesque."

But President Kennedy, as masterful as his group of assistants and "keepers of the image-flame" were, was not without detractors. He has often been described as high on style, big on image, light on substance. Whether loved or hated, his election and term of office marked a definite turning point in campaign imagery.

But in more current times, pundits and muckrakers so thoroughly dissect the personal lives and records of candidates and officeholders at every level that it is virtually impossible to avoid scrutiny that will suggest *some* wrongdoing at some point. And, by the standards of tabloid journalism, if a record is totally clear, that too becomes reason for suspicion.

In Theodore H. White's award-winning book *The Making of a President, 1960,* scrupulous attention to detail was paid to matters of minutiae from haircuts to necktie patterns to the color of campaign rally backdrops and curtains. Speeches were fine-tuned so they boomed and echoed with buzzwords and "action" verbs, though nothing of substance was committed to.

Joe McGinnis' book *The Selling of the President 1968* described the comeback and election of Richard Nixon. Following his defeat in 1960, Mr. Nixon learned about the importance of images from his victorious opponent and next time around drew his chief aides from the J. Walter Thompson ad agency.

From the jacket of Mr. McGinnis' book, he asks, "How do you correct a candidate's lack of humor and warmth? When does a candidate need 'more memorable phrases'? What is a 'balanced' television panel?

"These are just a few of the considerations that went into Richard Nixon's 1968 presidential campaign—at the heart of which was the adroit use and manipulation of television.

". . . Nixon had learned bitterly the importance of television. . . . One of his first moves in putting together a team for the 1968 campaign was the appointment of a seasoned team of advertising and TV professionals."

Packaging has become so important that a candidate hoping to succeed begins with a package "wrap": the New Deal, the New Frontier, the Great Society, Morning in America, the New Covenant. . . . In battle, one American leader used the package wrap "Operation Desert Shield" and "Operation Desert Storm" to help portray himself as a warrior while shocking much of the country by feeling he needed to state publicly that he was "not a wimp."

President Gerald Ford's "WIN" campaign, for Whip Inflation Now, proved an embarrassment.

A package wrap served the Republican Party in the 1994 elections, when it presented its "Contract with America," a list of what it would do if elected. The strategy was an inspired one—and, it turned out, a winning one—in that it amounted to little more than a list of those things the Republicans had been pushing all along. "Re-wrapping" the message and calling it a "contract" gave it a more solemn, serious sense of importance and value. By believing they were the other party to the contract, voters could embrace the concept and become a seemingly more involved part of the process. Details and nuances, such as how the contract's provisions would be funded, were waved aside for the time being, as that would have complicated the simplicity of the idea. The packaging concept, the wrap, was the key.

In 1995, religious conservatives offered a "Contract with the American Family," a list of items that the religious right had been pushing for some 20 years. But the new packaging was a reason to call a press conference and sound a rallying cry.

A better-educated, more sophisticated electorate and a more technologically advanced and competitive press corps has taken the decision making out of the smoke-filled rooms that character-ized politics for decades. Out in a more open setting, image takes on added significance and first impressions count. The Kennedy Family, it has often been said, is the closest thing America has to a royal family. Their carefully cultured and protected image has enhanced their own opportunities and privilege over the years. Even after tragedy and outrageous errors in judgment, the family still finds respect and reverence accorded years after the first strong figures made their mark.

When a well-cultured image becomes tarnished, some get a second chance and others don't.

Senator Gary Hart was a front runner for his party's presi-dential nomination. When accused of behaving inappropriately in public with a fashion model, he denied wrongdoing, refused to dignify the matter with comment . . . and, politically, was finished.

In contrast, Governor Bill Clinton in an almost identical situation, summoned his dignity and, with his wife at his side, told a television interviewer he hadn't been an angel, but was not about to be blackmailed into quitting public service. He went on to become President of the United States.

Senator Ted Kennedy never really gave a plausible explanation of circumstances surrounding a young woman's death while she was in his company, so his political advancement was short-circuited.

Senator Charles Robb apologized to his wife and the voters of his state on network TV for being in a hotel room alone with a beauty queen who said she'd given him a massage. His apology appeared sincere, was accepted . . . and he won reelection, coming from behind in the polls.

It's been said politics is a dirty business. This is a marketing book and not an attempt to reform the political system. People won't stop calling each other names and showing their opponents' dirty laundry if they believe it will help them get ahead. A presentation on ethics, honesty, integrity and just pointing out the merit of your side seems more simplistic than this arena is likely to embrace.

But for the public figure seeking to create or change perceptions, the recommendations to the politician, the lawyer, the doctor and the clergyman all follow the same formula plan.

- Analyze your situation honestly.
- Create realistic objectives for what you want to achieve.
- Develop a strategy and tactics to achieve your objectives.
- Define your USP—your unique selling proposition; what makes you worthy of your constituent audience's patronage, loyalty, support, trust, reference or vote; what's the benefit to them?

When these four points are addressed realistically, a plan to create, change or nurture an image is evolving. If misrepresentations or wishful thinking are any part of your response to these points, the plan may still be possible and may even succeed smashingly. The risk of exposure, however, hangs over your head and holds the potential to not only sink your plan and obliterate your goals, but leave a residue of mistrust of those in your profession and your industry that could linger for generations.

Image marketing seeks to publicize the best and most positive things that you do. Negatives aren't concealed, they are revealed, but in a context of, hopefully, a larger more encompassing display of positives and a reservoir of goodwill. That the total picture will leave perceptions of far more positives than negatives is the essence of the image you create and which, itself, becomes a positive focus point.

AT A GLANCE: WHEN THE PRODUCT IS BIGGER THAN A BREADBOX

1. To marketers, "a product" can be anything including an entire industry, a profession, a city, a country, a political or social cause, an entertainer or a candidate for public office.
2. Professions such as doctors, lawyers and accountants have historically believed marketing in general and advertising in particular was undignified and cheapened the image of their respective professions. It is now, however, a part of most of their annual operating budgets.
3. A problem with some of the military's image ads was that they sought to change people's perceptions without addressing the issues that were the underlying concerns.
4. To promote the military's image, ads should show and tell what today's military services do well; dispel myths and misconceptions; tell the public *why* it should be supportive; and position a single spokesperson who will make points and take questions, in contrast to perceptions of a sprawling and confused bureaucracy.
5. When the image of the institution is under fire, tell your story first—don't let others define your problem; talk about positive things you're doing; create goodwill;

be honest; correct your mistakes. Remember that the public tends to be open minded and forgiving of one who errs, apologizes, and promises to correct the problem.

6. Churches tend to do well by doing good in their communities, in contrast to televangelists and modern churches that focus on contemporary entertainment to fill the pews. People have many choices for entertainment, but what they seek—and find—in a church should be reflected in its image.

7. Institutions of higher learning should set and maintain standards. Those that quickly alter their focus and offer accommodations in the name of political correctness undermine the image to which they aspire and which theoretically reflects their principles.

8. Schools individually need to create their images based on their individual uniqueness. Designations like *institute* and *center* help to define such images.

9. Collectively schools need to have a plan to counter images attributed to all schools. When a particular controversy erupts at one school, it must not be perceived as a reflection of all.

10. Cities and towns that advertise themes and slogans such as "We're the best" are preaching to the choir. Tourists and businesses want to know why they should care about a place, much less support it.

11. Businesses and travellers are impressed with value and benefits such as tax incentives and discounts on services and support as much as they are with location and quality of life.

12. Promoting the numbers of schools, parks, lakes, museums, and the area's commitment to art and commerce in a message offers reasons to visit and to stay.

13. Too often, doctors and lawyers are perceived as arrogant and uncaring. Show some humility; listen to people's concerns; be cautious and always remember who it is that's paying for your services; charge fairly as

the big bills are not necessarily reflective of big or
better service; check your ego at the door—being
confident of your talent is great, being insensitive and
unresponsive is not; devote a part of each week to pro
bono services; guarantee your work—not the outcome,
just the quality of services rendered.

14. Packaging of programs can be a successful, but risky
technique: The New Deal, New Frontier and Contract
with America were successful "package wraps." The
Great Society and WIN (Whip Inflation Now) were not.
People are becoming more sophisticated and sensitized
to catchphrases, buzzwords and soundbites that all
sound good, but deliver little.

15. Image Marketing presents the positives and the
negatives in a context that emphasizes the positives
and acts of goodwill so that the resulting image is
honest as well as, on balance, favorable.

The Negative Option

Without actually doing the research, let's assume for the sake of argument that our earliest political campaigns were every bit as nasty as modern campaigns. Let's assume that the eloquent statements that begin, "My distinguished worthy opponent . . ." and end ". . . is a liar, a snake and a thief" have a long history. To make such assumptions explains why in modern campaigns, for all the superior education, intelligence and sophistication, candidates and their managers still continue to opt, early on, for a "negative campaign."

In corporate meetings and advertising, it's not a lot more mannerly. In the battle to be the customer's preferred long-distance phone service, AT&T and MCI make no pretense of subtle references to "the other guy." *Both* companies refer to the other by name, and each claims the other consistently lies about the costs and hidden "conditions" to get discounts or lower rates. Visa and American Express have set aside that stuffy banker image long enough to dump on one another as well.

Not only is the public confused about the name calling and accusations, the overall image left behind is that *no one is being straight with the consumer.*

Tylenol ran ad campaigns saying it was the choice of doctors and hospitals over aspirin, but, to its credit, it never singled out a particular *brand* of aspirin as the bad choice. . . . Until Advil started claiming *it* by name was the preferred choice over Tylenol by name. Apparently seeing the handwriting on the wall, Excedrin, Bayer aspirin, Nuprin and any number of other pain relievers began positioning their brands as not just products with intrinsic value, but in name comparison with all competitors.

And not unlike the AT&T/MCI messages, each appeared to have the evidence to *prove* it was superior in its class, which may help to explain, in these cynical times, why people increasingly are skeptical of research studies.

The Pepsi Challenge, that very successful 1974 comparison taste test, pitted Pepsi-Cola against not some generic brand or Cola-X, but Coca-Cola, the historic market leader. To no one's surprise, Pepsi was the brand of choice in test after test.

Was it?

Well, it *said* it was. Coke dismissed the matter and the public regarded the whole business as a lot of competitive posturing by the two rival market leaders, while market analysts and retailers didn't take it all that seriously. But that was okay with Pepsi because the brand received a lot of attention and, after all, that was the point.

Comparison testing, taste or otherwise, has pretty much always been with us. The phrase "shop and compare" is a part of the advertising lexicon. But to market one's product or advance one's image, how far is it appropriate to go in directing your inclusion of a competitor in your efforts by name when the references are negative?

While that was pretty much a rhetorical question, the answer seems to be go as far as you want to—all's fair in love, war and product advertising.

In politics, it is increasingly popular to run not only negative references to opponents, but what is termed "attack" ads. These ads usually mention the candidate benefitting from the ad only at the very end, with the words "paid for by the committee to elect _____." The entire ad content then is totally an attack on the record or the character (or *both*) of the opposition candidate.

There are people who believe this approach is nasty, vicious, mean-spirited and certainly unsportsmanlike. Many people believe "attack ads" suggest a certain degree of desperation—that a candidate will sink to any level to gain an advantage.

Massachusetts Governor Michael Dukakis was regarded as perhaps one of the weakest candidates the Democratic party had offered for president in many elections. Still, it was the George Bush campaign's "Willie Horton ad," which charged Governor Dukakis with having a lenient attitude on crime, that was the most remembered, vicious and *effective* ad of the campaign. Few people would suggest that the ad represented Mr. Bush's finest hour. No one, however, disputes its effectiveness.

The charge that attack ads and negative campaigns that trash competitors are ill-advised because they seek to appeal to the public's most base instincts is dismissed by those who believe, in a highly-charged competitive environment, whatever it takes to get the job done is fair. To attack a political foe is represented as a sign of strength—a simple "law of the jungle/survival of the fittest" technique. On the corporate side, if the objective is to sell a lot of product, to be a viable factor in the market and to gain market share, the idea of naming and dismissing a competitor or its product is merely a function of aggressive positioning.

Clearly, to people of this mindset, references to ethics, morality, and dignity belong in the file with old news. Remember the jungle?

A fundamental premise of marketing is that, if the best thing you can say about your product is something negative about your competition, your product has a problem.

Clarence Peterson, writing in the *Chicago Tribune,* noted, "Logical argument has all but disappeared from political discourse, much of it replaced by what [Professor Ray] Perkins calls 'ad hominem' attacks, also known as character assassination, attack politics or smears." Professor Perkins had written a book called *Logic and Mr. Limbaugh,* in which he criticized the positions of the wildly popular talk show host Rush Limbaugh as being basically arguments based on a flawed premise from the standpoint of a logician. Those positions were notoriously loud and negative. Advocates for the opposite position would argue that Mr. Limbaugh holds sway over a large and loyal constituent audience that has put many millions of dollars in his pockets, buying his books, tapes, videos, newsletters, coffee mugs, neckties, attending his lectures and supporting his television and radio programs.

The argument is that if you are that successful, not only do you not have a reason to change, but that you would be a fool to do so. Whether Mr. Limbaugh, for his part is a genuine right wing idealogue or merely an entertainer is irrelevant for purposes of this example. He has defined his image—loud, angry, abrasive—a bulldozer in a business suit—and the image has connected. Observers offer that before Mr. Limbaugh was the talk (or shout) of the town, a similar boisterous success was the talk show host Morton Downey Jr., who came on strong, soared like a proverbial rocket, sort of fizzled out there in space and hasn't been heard from in years—not that he hasn't tried. The angry, desk-pounding, mad-as-hell-and-I'm-not-going-to-take-it-anymore spokesperson for "the little guy" historically gets a lot of attention, only to wear out his welcome and become a bit of a bore.

On the other side of the spectrum, the National Organization for Women (NOW) tried to seize the moment—an opportunity— it believed would gain greater attention for itself and its cause by attacking Mr. Limbaugh for *his* negativism regarding their agenda. NOW released a series of attacks, culminating in a bumbling attempt to organize a boycott of Mr. Limbaugh's sponsors. The boycott failed; NOW looked foolish; Mr. Limbaugh continued to bluster and the entire episode ranks as a textbook example of pointless, childish name-calling on a national scale.

In *Spin Control,* a fine book by John Anthony Maltese, a memo from the files of President Richard Nixon's White House Chief of Staff, H.R. Haldeman, states, "The President is especially anxious that your group . . . set up a system of furnishing attack material on a daily basis to a group of key people [who] will be lining up to be our first line of battle for the Administration."

The years since have seen a great deal written about such activities in President Nixon's White House. While history will credit him with major accomplishments, particularly in the area of foreign policy, he will always be remembered above all else as the first U.S. President to resign in disgrace. Terms such as "dirty tricks" and "enemies list" are forever linked to his presidency. The members of his administration, dismissed at the time as "a cadre of PR men," were immensely effective . . . until they were sent to prison.

Rance Crain wrote in *Advertising Age,* "Don't hold your breath that politicians the next time around will rely any less on negative advertising, or that marketers, during the next Olympics, will forsake 'ambush' marketing tactics. The simple reason, of course, is they work."

Maybe. But how effective is negative marketing over the long haul? Without carrying the practice to where one ends up in jail, it is worth noting those instances where such strategies have, in hindsight, been deemed ill-chosen approaches, at best.

To accentuate the positive may seem like a quaint or anti-quated idea at a time when Robert Hughes' *The Culture of Complaint* sits fixed on national best-seller lists and *The New York Times* describes singer John Denver's songs as "pastoral reveries that have lost their footing in a pop mainstream increasingly obsessed with paranoia and complaint."

These are *songs* they're talking about!

So the songs are rough, the politics is rough and the business jungle is still a jungle.

But the best times—the times people ultimately choose to remember—are filled with those images they choose to keep and surround themselves with. The ads you'll want to frame and hang on your walls won't likely be attack ads. The speeches or comments you will want to be remembered for will very likely not be the ones heavy with complaints, insults, negativism and attacks on your competition.

The 1980s saw scores of successful "support groups" forming, many of them made up of people who found comfort in character-izing themselves as "victims."

To be a marketer in such a climate can be particularly chal-lenging; to create and maintain a positive image is undermined by negativism—regardless of where it is directed.

For a giant such as AT&T to spend major ad dollars telling people what's wrong with MCI gives major exposure to MCI at AT&T's expense. That would seem to make a strong case for bringing back "Brand X" or, better still, focusing simply on what AT&T is doing well and right and let the competition keep punching at the wind. When AT&T takes the punch, who wins? Not the confused customer certainly.

When McDonald's offered one of its most successful ad themes in "You deserve a break today," an overworked, tired public responded with a sigh, a smile and a "thank you."

If success in marketing comes from telling your audience *what's in it for them,* then stick to telling them just that. Throwing in a little name-calling can and frequently *does* backfire. That benefits no one. Remember, if you can't say something nice about someone, particularly *yourself,* your problem is bigger than marketing.

AT A GLANCE: THE NEGATIVE OPTION

1. Referring to your competitors by name gives them publicity at your expense.
2. People tend to be suspicious of people who trash other people or products to advance their own interests.
3. If the best thing you can say about yourself or your company is something negative about your competition, you have a serious problem regarding your company or yourself.
4. People want to know what's in it for them. Present your benefits and leave competitors who use attack ads and comparison ads to punch at the wind. Once you begin answering their attacks by attacking *them,* it doesn't prove strength, it proves vulnerability.
5. Helping raise the visibility of a competitor—and perhaps invite a sympathetic response for the competitor—by going on the attack and naming competitors in your ads, is a poor allocation of your marketing budget.

The Image Marketing Casebook

The Image Marketing Casebook

Some enterprises have existed—even *expanded*—based on just being the image of success, when the reality may have been absent or, to be generous, slow to catch up. Donald Trump, for example, was able to keep his creditors at bay and even borrow more while he was reportedly considerably overextended. While some of his real estate developments had obviously been quite successful, master self-promoter that he was, it was his personal image as the suave, tuxedo-clad dealmaker, photographed nightly at an opening or charity function, in the company of New York's power elite, that conveyed the impression that he, himself, wielded that power and was, thus, creditworthy.

Lee Iacocca and John Sculley, on the other hand, were men of considerable substance, CEOs with the great track records. Just to hear that they were being consulted, much less "on board," was enough to calm most nervous boards of directors and reassure the banks.

The newest perfume from Calvin Klein, sandwich from McDonald's or ice cream flavor from Ben & Jerry's takes success as a given, basking comfortably in the image of a consistent winner.

Yet, despite the vision, intelligence, imagination and spirit that have made Ted Turner, Apple Computer and Playboy forces who have created, defined or revolutionized their respective signature ventures, each new prospect is greeted with the same reserve, apprehension and skepticism as the first.

Chalk it up to image.

Whether the subject is a person, a thing, a place or a corporation, the image it projects is what will be remembered and evaluated.

Mr. Sculley holds a Wharton School MBA and *looks* as if he does; Mr. Iacocca is the image of the wise, experienced father-figure; Mr. Turner appears to relish being characterized as a maverick, though his cowboy-in-the-boardroom image has made Wall Street nervous more than once and has made it harder for him to achieve his goals. Playboy developed a reputation as a company whose reach exceeded its grasp: being a successful publisher of a sophisticated magazine doesn't (and didn't) guarantee one can profitably run hotels, and movie companies.

The Walt Disney Company has a business history that sometimes resembles a ride on Space Mountain. Perhaps the most successful merchandising and licensing operation of all time, the corporation's list of unsuccessful ventures shows that there were times the mouse with the golden touch fumbled. Yet, its winning image allows every new Disney venture to be greeted, for better or worse, with breathless anticipation. Here are some of the most successful images . . . and some that are not:

APPLE COMPUTER
John Sculley
Steve Jobs

Most visible media: print, TV, PR

By the summer of 1995, Apple Computer, John Sculley and Steve Jobs were not actively involved with one another professionally. Yet, the history as well as the future fortunes of the three would be forever interrelated.

Having dropped out of college, Steve Jobs was designing video games for Atari in 1972. He sold his Volkswagen to get money for computer parts a few years later when he (with fellow computer buff Steve Wozniak) started Apple in the garage and a bedroom of his parents' home. Six years later, Apple Computer was a Fortune 500 company, with 1982 sales of more than $583 million.

Steve Jobs hardly looked like a computer company executive with his mustache, sideburns, western shirts and faded jeans. The computer industry was still relatively young and esoteric, and Mr. Jobs' look and nontraditional style helped contribute to his emerging image as a visionary, a maverick and a genius—or at least a "boy wonder."

And in the folklore of business, the title of "boy wonder" was taken very seriously. Every profession and industry had a few. Almost always, they could be counted on to be admired, respected and envied. Almost always, they could be counted on to go after the giant of the industry and threaten a showdown.

In the computer industry, the giant was IBM. When Apple could boast $1.5 billion in sales, IBM had $40 billion. When Apple's net income was an impressive $64 million, IBM's was a staggering $6.6 billion.

Yet, Apple was the image of vision and entrepreneurship. When Steve Jobs courted John Sculley to be Apple's CEO, Sculley was the President of Pepsi-Cola. After 16 years with Pepsi, he was regarded as something of a "boy wonder" himself. As the cover of John Sculley's book, *Odyssey: Pepsi to Apple . . . The Journey of a Marketing Impresario,* tells it, "John Sculley, at age 38, had been Pepsi's youngest president when he rewrote the rules of marketing, masterminding the "Pepsi Generation" campaign. . . . Compelled by Apple's fabulous success and co-founder Steve Jobs' promise of 'a chance to change the world,' Sculley turned his back on East Coast corporate orthodoxy and joined the high-risk, gold rush atmosphere of Silicon Valley."

Humility not withstanding, separately and together, Mr. Jobs and Mr. Sculley have done some things both very right and very wrong from a marketing standpoint. Clearly, luck, timing and fine products had much to do with the success. Ego had a lot to do with the missteps.

Apple's TV commercial "1984," shown only once during the Super Bowl, proved to be the most talked-about television commercial of the year and for some time after that. Another PR coup was getting every seat in the stadium to have a seat cushion bearing the Apple logo—a stunt, to be sure, but bright and the subject of more than visual interest on TV screens around the world.

Business Week has called Steve Jobs and John Sculley "The Dynamic Duo."

In *Odyssey,* Mr. Sculley wrote that the Silicon Valley was like

> a corporate Camelot: Apple was its Round Table and Steve was its King Arthur. . . . I had led the creation of "a Pepsi Generation" . . . Then, Steve called. Like so many others, I bought into the dream of this precocious, mesmerizing kid.
>
> Together—he as chairman and me as chief executive—we would become the unbeatable team to put a personal computer into almost every home and every classroom and, in so doing, change the world. I was to create an "Apple Generation" and find new markets for the company's "insanely great" products.
>
> What I discovered at Apple was a community without boundaries. A free-form environment, an artists' workshop. . . . We fiercely competed on a tenth of a percent of the market share. And we sold what Steve disdainfully called sugared water.

From such vision—and hyperbole—the team steered Apple to be seen as David to IBM's Goliath. In that story, of course, David prevailed, toppling the giant. The stone that these visionaries saw making it happen would be the Macintosh computer—or something like it. Mr. Sculley wrote that the launch of the Mac was event marketing "which was one of the most thoroughly planned and comprehensive consumer marketing programs ever assembled":

> The event became key. Every release of information about the product centered on a celebration of Apple and its vision. Through a convergence of advertising, promotion and public relations, the experience of the event would have to match the experience of the product.
>
> Macintosh's launch was a success and other successes followed with Mr. Sculley carrying his Pepsi hype, promotion and analogies onward, touting this time not "refreshment for the body, but tools for the mind."

But carbonated beverages have been known to lose their fizz and machines break down. Mr. Sculley noted that one day they were the "Dynamic Duo" and the next "unable to get anything right. Our sales dropped with our hopes. A computer slump, the long shadow of IBM, a mixture of poor judgment and bad luck—and Apple Computer had plunged into a severe crisis. All of it occurred with dramatic suddenness."

Each man tried to remove the other from power. The company that had so determinedly sought the spotlight now found the whole world watching as John Sculley wrestled control of the now bobbing Apple from its founder. Steve Jobs, the visionary—King Arthur—was ousted.

John Sculley calls the story of Apple a "gospel of innovation." With Steve Jobs jettisoned in 1985, Mr. Sculley focused on software development and a more structured, business-like environment in which he sought to take Apple into the twenty-first century. In 1993, Mr. Sculley, somewhat abruptly, himself departed the company. Months later, Mr. Sculley announced he would become CEO of Dallas-based Spectrum Information Technologies—and four months later resigned that position, filing a suit against its owners, who in turn, sued him for breach of contract.

Steve Jobs, out of his cowboy shirt and jeans, in a business suit and looking more like a college professor than a college student, announced the creation of Next Computer in 1985 to much fanfare. In 1993, he abandoned its original computer hardware business, saying it would focus on software. *Information Week* magazine reported that "It seemed as if Jobs' shining star . . . had crashed and burned." However, the story noted that deals with Chrysler, Mobil and McCaw Cellular Communications had won some respect for Mr. Jobs, who may be turning things around. To an entire generation of techies, Steve Jobs may have been brash, arrogant and abrasive, but he was, and is, a visionary whose time has not run out.

And Apple? The computer company with the grand, romantic vision and the plan to change the world appears to continue to sputter and stumble. With much of its hope for the future riding on the acceptance of "Newton," a personal communicator, it looked as if the Apple might be close to rotting on the tree.

One year after Newton's introduction, *Advertising Age* noted, "Apple Computer's much-hyped and much ridiculed Newton personal communicator will be one year old . . . and Apple finally seems to appreciate the gravity of its mistakes." An Apple spokesman acknowledged: "The fundamental problem that we had with Newton was a hype problem. We learned our lesson."

Indeed.

Two weeks later, another *Ad Age* story sought to offer advice to John Sculley and Apple regarding Newton and their respective selves: "Get a vision check-up. Mr. Sculley, caught up in his vision of the future, over-promised and over-promoted. No product could have lived up to that billing."

So a bright star in technology and two very bright talents (at least) seem to have been badly burned by a series of "hype problems." Vision is important and imagination is both wonderful and admirable. But when David takes his eyes off Goliath in order to read his press notices and become filled with a sense of self-importance, his star can fizzle and burn out quite quickly.

BEN & JERRY'S
Most visible media: point-of-sale, PR

Ice cream is not a necessity of life. It is a dessert. And, if anyone in the scientific or medical community is to be believed, not an altogether healthy dessert at that.

Yet consumers consume ice cream at increasing rates year after year, making it a multi-billion dollar business.

Ben & Jerry's ice cream is high in butterfat, costs more than many other brands, and is hugely successful. Much of their marketing is image marketing. The company's mission statement is this:

> Ben & Jerry's is dedicated to the creation and demonstration of a new corporate concept of linked prosperity. Our mission consists of three interrelated parts.
>
> Product Mission: To make, distribute and sell the finest quality all natural ice cream and related products in a wide variety of innovative flavors made from Vermont dairy products.

Social Mission: to operate the company in a way that recognizes the central role that business plays in the structure of society by initiating innovative ways to improve the quality of life of a broad community, local, national and international.

Economic Mission: To operate the company on a sound financial basis of profitable growth, increasing value for our shareholders and creating career opportunities and financial rewards for our employees.

Underlying the mission of Ben & Jerry's is the determination to seek new and creative ways of addressing all three parts, while holding a deep respect for individuals inside and outside the company of which they are part.

Whew!

First, as mission statements go, Ben & Jerry's is about ten times longer than most, which are usually a few sentences. Second, it's not funny. Fred "Chico" Lager, a former CEO of Ben & Jerry's Ice Cream, wrote about the company and its principals (and principles) in a book titled *Ben & Jerry's: The Inside Scoop.* Its subtitle promised to speak to that which most people found distinctly different about the operation. It was *How Two Real Guys Built a Business with a Social Conscience and a Sense of Humor.*

Mr. Lager writes "Ben & Jerry's image and marketing approach was exactly the opposite of everyone else's. If Häagen-Dazs and the clones were worldly and elegant, we were funky and unpretentious. Ben & Jerry's was down-home and genuine."

While initially coming to market with some interesting, if not exciting, flavor combinations, it was the sense of humor brought to bear on naming later flavors that brought the point of departure in the retailers' freezers and caught the interest and fascination of the public:

- "Cherry Garcia" (in both ice cream and low fat frozen yogurt), a spoof on the name of The Grateful Dead guitarist Jerry Garcia, to whom a royalty is paid, a portion of which goes to a foundation.

- "Rainforest Crunch," a portion of the profits from this flavor go to preserve and save the rain forests, as well as various environmental and peace groups.

- "Aztec Harvests Coffee" flavor uses product from a company "owned by Mexico's self-directed coffee co-operatives (which) gives coffee farmers direct access to the marketplace and funds projects helping Mexico's rural farm communities."

The packaging is bold, colorful and artistic and carries a note that purchasers are getting a good quality product and "helping to raise the standard of living of small rural farmers, too." Other flavors, such as "Chubby Hubby," "Coffee Toffee Crunch" and "Bluesberry" not only get attention and a smile at the point-of-sale, but carry the message: "Put up or call up! 1 out of 4 kids in the U.S. is born into poverty. Together we can help them! Call 1-800-BJ KIDS-1."

The Call for Kids campaign, the Rain Forests, Increase the Peace—Ben & Jerry's campaign against hand guns—the Children's Defense Fund, and the help for rural farmers are causes that result in Ben & Jerry's being profiled and interviewed as the media sees them as model corporate citizens, not just ice cream merchants. Their belief is that the company can influence society through its communications with its customers. Customers are also supposed to feel good about buying a brand that helps people. Even a higher priced brand.

Mr. Lager quotes Ben & Jerry's founder, Ben Cohen, proposing to "redefine the bottom line" to include both an economic and social component. "We can't just optimize profits, we need to optimize the community as well."

In 1995, Ben & Jerry's was valued as a $150 million company through potential licensing opportunities, according to *Advertising Age*.

A number of companies in its industry have the reputation of producing quality products, but Ben & Jerry's stands out as being the one with the "social conscience and the sense of humor," both of which they are putting to use for maximum marketing potential.

Politically, socially, environmentally, medically there seems to be no obvious justification for the phenomenal success of Ben & Jerry's, other than perhaps the mantra of the 1980s: "I deserve this!" So, after a grueling period of deprivation in the name of

better health, indulgence and a professed appreciation for quality—indeed *excellence*—in a pseudo-food dessert became more than
acceptable. It became an act of defiance, independence and a
reflection of success—a reward, if you will. It was positioned at a
time and for a group who believed the time for self-indulgence had
come. And for those who brought a conscience, Ben & Jerry's
brought a cause.

BENETTON
Most visible media: print, outdoor, collateral

Sometimes preparing a critical analysis of a company's public
image is too easy. That's certainly the case if the company appears
to be overtly—blatantly—trying to shock or offend. That certainly
appears to be the case with the Italian clothing company Benetton.

Rance Crain, in a 1994 *Advertising Age* column, wrote:

> Spare me from companies that wear their marketing programs
> on their sleeves. What they're trying to show, of course, is that
> they possess more social consciousness than their competitors,
> but the net effect to me is that they don't have anything to say
> about what really matters and that's their products and how
> they'll help consumers.
>
> Benetton, as an example, goes to extremes to avoid talking
> about [or showing] its overpriced clothing. If you're not outraged
> about their ad showing a priest kissing a nun, all you have to
> do is wait for the next even more outrageous rendition.

Indeed, Mr. Crain goes on to describe other Benetton ads and
an edition of the company's quarterly magazine, which he says
"successfully makes the transition from tasteless to disgusting."

Several months later, in another issue of *Advertising Age*,
Dagmar Mussey wrote from Dusseldorf, Germany: "Benetton's
advertising shot heard 'round the world may be recoiling on the
controversial clothier."

Such criticism would seem, however, to be perhaps expected,
if not desired, considering the lengths to which the company appears

ready to go to be outrageous. And with all the controversy, outrage and the attacks, what effect has it all had on Benetton?

Business appears to be excellent with worldwide 1994 sales estimated at $2 billion.

The advertising campaign theme "United Colors of Benetton" indeed rarely shows the company's product and routinely shocks the viewer, whether ads appear in magazines or on billboards. In Germany, in 1995, the campaign was banned completely. Curiously, nowhere does the Benetton name even appear on the front or back covers or the spine of its own magazine. What *does* appear are teasers for stories inside: Sports! (for sissies); train surfing in Rio; toilet bowl tossing in California; naked men vs. naked women . . . to name a few. The headline on page eight of one issue asks, "What the hell *is* this magazine?" The printed answer is, "To be honest, we're figuring it out as we go along." The 147-page issue *does* have one Benetton ad (showing only a hand holding flowers) amid several pages of photographs of naked people.

Outrageous photographs certainly can get attention. Pretend it's artistic, but it's really a very old and cheap route to getting noticed.

So they are profitable. But what is the image Benetton is attempting to create for itself with these ads, magazines and billboards? If the company has a long-term plan, it's not telling. It professes to have a social conscience, so it lampoons religious hypocrisy and raises public awareness of disease and injustice. And, as Rance Crain points out, this all has nothing to do with the manufacture or sale of its product.

True, the company's image is evolving as *bold, gutsy, independent, irreverent, outrageous,* but does it serve its own ends to be called tasteless and offensive? And do a majority of people exposed to their message even know that Benetton is a clothing store? Does this sort of thing sell sweaters? How long until, segment by segment, the company will have offended and alienated every part of the market?

A Benetton Foundation carrying the torch for the social issues might be a more directly effective approach, while a marketing effort that speaks to the value of its product might help continue selling clothes. Creative cutting-edge advertising does not need to be drab or offensive. Igniting passion by itself does not solve problems—or sell clothes.

To date, Benetton's marketing image suggests an overindulged rich kid in a candy store, attracting a lot of attention, but with a big stomach ache in the foreseeable future.

THE BODY SHOP
Most visible media: point-of-sale; collateral; PR

You say you'd rather be right than be rich?

Anita Roddick will settle for both—being very much at peace with her conscience, doing her part for the environment and raking in the profits at the same time. As a marketer, her approach is decidedly nontraditional, and that's by design. The image she and her company project is every bit as calculated in its advancement as if the most sophisticated agency had carried her flag.

In 1976, Anita Roddick opened her first Body Shop store, insisting she would never hire an ad agency and would never advertise. By the fall of 1994, she had fudged a bit on her promises, having hired the London ad agency Chiat/Day as "strategic communications consultants" and having produced a thirty-minute television infomercial.

One can split hairs over such promises, but the bottom line is a much more dramatic story: retail sales in 1994 of some $666 million, with pre-tax profits of $43.5 million from more than 1,100 stores in 45 countries.

While the Body Shop may not have followed the standard advertising procedures, there are those very lavish store windows and Ms. Roddick as the subject of a good deal more media attention during a typical year than CEOs of companies that *do* advertise in the traditional ways.

The reason she is able to garner so much media interest is only passingly due to her heading up a company that purports to sell "all natural" products from soaps to shampoo to facial cleansers and accessories. She presents herself as a passionate environmentalist, strongly opposed to animal testing, who pours money earned in her business into her social causes. In virtually every story ever produced on The Body Shop, the phrases "sells natural products, eschews animal testing and spends no money on advertising" appears with enough consistency to seem like a mantra or, at least, a part of the logo.

Anita Roddick has crafted an image for herself and her company as a bold, aggressive, unconventional, outspoken and righteous—sometimes, rather self-righteous in the view of critics. Far from following the adage of "the customer is always right," she will tell you her opinions and her philosophy without waiting to be asked—and if you don't agree with her, you are free to buy your shampoo elsewhere.

Indeed, product literature racks in a typical Body Shop store are stuffed with pamphlets and tracts with titles such as "The Body Shop approach against animal testing" and "What on earth are we doing?" The latter piece includes this information: "The Body Shop celebrates Earth Day everyday, year-round with a variety of practices and programs including: careful sourcing (. . . t-shirt is printed by City Works, a micro-enterprise dedicated to creating jobs for the unemployed in inner-city Washington, D.C. Ingredients in The Body Shop are sourced with equal care, taking into account environmental, social and animal welfare issues) Environmental Management Practices . . . Community Service . . . Wind Farm (. . . farm in Wales generates electricity to compensate for some of the energy we use in production), Tree Planting . . . Reuse, Refill, Recycle."

Even the more nearly-traditional product literature, such as a piece titled "Hair—Who Needs It?" includes a section headed "The Tyranny of Fashion."

Some would hold that The Body Shop and its founder carefully cultivate an image rich in controversy in order to get attention. Is the objective promoting environmental awareness, social conscience or selling cosmetics? Can't it legitimately be all of them?

The answer is, of course, it can.

But if books such as this one urge that you view everything you do, from your letterhead to your packaging, trucks and most random comments, as a potential marketing opportunity, The Body Shop has put that practice into play dramatically. Every printed piece carries as much a social message as a product message; and while so many product messages run together and sound like claims you've heard before, a message that is unique—even *unnerving*—is one you will remember. The Body Shop practices an "in-your-face" kind of marketing. Its CEO appears on TV programs such as cable's Comedy Central talk show "Politically Incorrect," in which she represents an image suggesting if people aren't prepared to be socially and environmentally responsible, she doesn't want them as customers. Clearly, this positioning will cause some people to dismiss her and shop elsewhere. But they will remember her. And the chances are they will never know the CEOs of her competitors' companies or even the companies themselves.

Is it important?

In a crowded business such as soaps, moisturizers and shampoos, product and brand awareness means shelf space, visibility and sales. It is also means share of mind/share of market.

In two issues of *Advertising Age,* a week apart, stories appeared with the headlines "Body Shop marches to its own drummer" and "Roddick skewers critics." Product visibility and a clearly defined image were advanced without an ad dollar spent. Love her or hate her, Anita Roddick has created an image she has marketed to tremendous success. She has used the very traditional elements of a standard marketing plan: traditional media (print, radio, TV collaterals), and traditional PR machinery to gain attention to promote a seemingly nontraditional image.

DISNEY
Most visible media: all

Being an American institution carries advantages and disadvantages relative to one's image. This is at least as true in the area of entertainment as it is with religion, the military, or politics.

A great number of books have been written about the Walt Disney Company, many of them published by the company itself. To consider the Disney image is to consider several images, clearly under an overall umbrella. As a provider of family entertainment, whether films, television, music, live shows or amusement parks, Disney is the very essence of wholesomeness—Snow White, Sleeping Beauty, Peter Pan, The Mickey Mouse Club and a seeming endless list that has something sure to appeal to everyone. As a business, Disney understands better than anyone the value of rights and ownership, having its own writers, artists, studio production facilities, distribution apparatus, book and music publishing and licensing units.

The Disney magic that began with cartoons, movies, a theme park and a television show has broadened its image to include its own Disney credit cards, time-share condos, and hotels and resorts.

Few companies have been so successful in so many fields. The Disney hotels are among the most successful convention as well as leisure travel sites. The Disney Channel is a successful cable television premium channel, getting a monthly fee from viewers above the basic cable TV charge.

Clearly, its founder, Walt Disney, deserves credit for having the vision to see what a cartoon could be and to carry its extensions to extremes few ever imagined possible.

Disney always retained ownership, but he managed to have it both ways. Items would be sold in the nationwide chain of Disney stores, but elsewhere as well. Original programming on the Disney Channel would be ultimately spun off to other TV outlets, home video—and back again, such as the series "Zorro," "Davy Crockett" and "The Mickey Mouse Club."

The Disney image—what it is and how it got there—is clear, obvious and upbeat when the company is riding the wave of success. In the 1990s, hit films like "Aladdin," "Beauty and the Beast," "The Lion King," and "Pocahontas" and top television shows like "Home Improvement," suggest the magic touch is intact. But only a decade earlier Disney films were proving to be box office disappointments, park attendance was off and "The Wonderful World of Disney" looked as if it might well become "a small world after all."

In mid-1995, *The New York Times* published a story headlined "Clouds Over Disneyland," in which it offered phrases like ". . . profits are still flowing, but the stability seems a blurred memory." Chairman Michael Eisner told shareholders at the company's

EXHIBIT 9.1

Walt Disney Company

These brochures are just one piece of the Disney marketing puzzle.

annual meeting that successful corporations often lose track of their mission: "Instead of the daring, nimble companies they once were, they become prisoners of their own success. Their pace becomes sluggish and their breathing labored. Decisions are made by committee and every bet must be a sure thing."

Disney's purchase of the film company Miramax, known for many rough, adult-oriented, decidedly un-Disney like films, seems like a hedge of sorts against future disappointments like EuroDisney. The day may still come, after all, when there won't be a "Lion King" to sell millions of dolls, toys, books, videos, tickets and clothing items.

Advertising Age, in 1994, offered that there was "New magic needed for Disney Kingdom." A Paine Webber securities analyst, Christopher Dixon, noted, "Disney continues to be the number one brand in entertainment. Every six-year-old on the planet knows. . . . The challenge is to demonstrate that [the theme parks are] not just for six-year-olds."

The strategy Disney appears ready to employ is to try to be all things to all people.

Adult action films and comedies will be released through subsidiaries Miramax, Touchstone, and Hollywood Pictures, while the Disney name itself will continue to be merchandised to six-year-olds of all ages in animated films, videos, books, music, toys and clothing.

The Disney image will always be for family entertainment, but newer ventures suggest that Wall Street may be looking at a more grown-up company in the twenty-first century. In addition to the very upscale hotels, Disney stores, those miniature magic kingdoms wedged into shopping malls everywhere, have a highly diversified literature rack. One brochure invites patrons to "Own a piece of the Magic" by purchasing time-share condos at the Disney Vacation club in Florida (with trade-offs "at more than 200 of the world's finest resorts"). Another brochure offers a "Gold Card" and a membership in the Magic Kingdom Club for $65 (for a two-year membership) that gets reduced prices at the Disney theme parks, stores, restaurants, shops, etc. Then there's the Disney Credit Card applications. While most retailers are throwing in the credit card towel and opting for Visa or Mastercard,

Disney has launched a credit card of its own that is honored . . . at the various Disney stores and properties. As Sears found, having a credit card base, while costly, returns a mailing list of gold.

The Disney Florida Vacation Tours brochure introduces again the great Disney World Theme Park and Disney–MGM Studios, as well as the lesser-known Disney's Fort Wilderness Resort and Campgrounds, Disney's Caribbean Beach Resort, Disney's Dixie Landings Resort, Disney's Yacht and Beach Club Resort and several more. And you thought you were just going to wear those ears in the tea cup ride all week long!

The Disney image is a double-edged sword. As long as attendance is good at the parks and hotels and a film or two a year hits it big, the perception will remain that everything with the Disney name on it is most likely to succeed. That a movie is a *Disney* movie is as important as the picture itself as a marketing factor. That's a point that Universal and 20th Century–Fox can't claim. The same holds true in most other areas where Disney competes as well. The name recognition factor often overwhelms.

Indeed, The Walt Disney Company's 1993 sales were $9.9 billion (up 17 percent) and net income $1.1 billion (up 24 percent). What's more, Disney put up these numbers in a year that park attendance was down. But another failure like EuroDisney, another procession of senior managers defecting, as happened in 1993–94, or a couple of disappointing films in a row (as happened in the early 1980s) can poison the well and create the perception that the company is on a losing streak. No one seems to want to back a loser. The benefit of having the Disney name on so many diversified projects, products and properties is that when most of them are doing well, they carry and/or support the others. But it works both ways. No one wants to play with the toy, see the film, buy the book or stay at the resort that no one else seems to want.

The Disney Company is highly visible in all media for all of its industries. If failure hits, such high visibility can be a short-term negative as it reminds everyone of the failure with which the company associates itself and undermines confidence in a project that may be fine. Such broad diversification as Disney now enjoys might best be represented clearly and distinctly as wholly separate entities, so a problem with one does not automatically cast a shadow over another. In any case, the image and the objectives, strategies and tactics relative to the success of the theme park, do not necessarily fit objectives, strategies, tactics and image that might fit a film company, publishing company, retail store or hotel. It is smart to want to extend the Disney "family" image across product lines, but be aware as, for example, Playboy Enterprises should have been, that what people want in a magazine is not necessarily the same thing people want in a hotel. Recognize the differences and speak to them.

Walt Disney used to say that his objective in everything he did was to educate and entertain. That philosophy applies nicely to the making of a cartoon, but gives one pause in the management of a resort or clothing line—and on a global level.

Some people used to ask about a particular Rockefeller brother: Is he the politician, the banker or foundation guy? The images might have been a bit blurred, the essence was that it was at least possible to maintain an image within an image. To be a part of the Disney family, but promote a distinction among its entities is a strategy that suggests basking in the light, but being prepared to distance one's self from the shadows.

HELMSLEY HOTELS
Leona Helmsley
Most visible media: print, PR

If all the public relations machinery in the United States had been brought to the cause of making Mrs. Leona Helmsley look bad, it could not match the level to which she dirtied herself—and several of New York's finest hotels as well.

As hotel chains go, images are generally positive—due in no small part to the various chains' efforts. Hyatt, Hilton, Marriott, Sheraton, Holiday Inn and others come in at various price ranges and suitability for meetings and conventions, business travel or family vacations. But mention Helmsley, and the image of the upscale, service-oriented hotel is eclipsed by the image of the woman herself. The woman one national magazine named to its "Hall of Shame," another called the "Queen of Mean." Among her misdeeds, she is alleged to have said that "taxes are for little people" before being sentenced to jail for tax evasion, and, upon release, having her employees perform her court-ordered community service work.

Before Mrs. Helmsley got into trouble and was reduced to tears in an unconvincing display for TV newswoman Barbara Walters (and apparently the judge, as well), she appeared in ads for Helmsley Hotels, calling herself "the Queen" and emphasizing her high standards. The ads were frequently satirized and were an embarrassment to the organization, but apparently, not to the lady herself. A 1995 ad in *The New Yorker* magazine, used the headline, "Say What You Will, She Runs a Helluva Hotel." The essence of the copy read, "At every Helmsley Hotel, a thousand and two details are completely polished, perfected and inspected to make sure we always satisfy you. And-you-know-who."

Indeed.

As if the ad by itself (and the frequent magazine and newspaper column items offering tidbits of lawsuits and unseemly behavior) weren't enough, the fine print, usually the work of the zealous corporate legal department, carries the reassuring line, "While Mrs. Helmsley doesn't personally operate or manage the Helmsley hotels, the high standards she has set are meticulously kept."

Perhaps there was a time that a bit of nose-in-the-air defiance or self-deprecating humor would have helped fill the rooms. But that time is gone. At least in this case. Since Mr. Helmsley became incapacitated, Mrs. Helmsley would have everyone believe she sets the tone, if not "personally operates, etc. . . ." And that's the problem. She casts a shadow, and a very dark one it is, across the properties.

If the ad in this example is true to the "Say What You Will . . . " then here goes: Say good-night, Mrs. Helmsley. Taking away the name, references or any illusion to an image that has so tarnished the properties will help them to remain viable in the very rate-and-amenity competitive hospitality industry. Whatever image the chain may choose to promote in the future, it is advisable to let go of the lingering ego and negative ties to the past. Reminders of Leona Helmsley are reminders of an extremely unpopular person whose very unpleasantness contributed to her fall from grace. Certainly, that is not an image to continue trying to market.

CHARLES SCHWAB
Most visible media: print, TV

The images that suggest investing and finance usually involve Wall Street stock tickers, street signs and tough-looking men in gray suits gesturing decisively. This is the money jungle, after all. It's no place for wimps. That one generic image has been used to present, at various times, the half-dozen or so major entities who have done any significant, high-profile advertising.

The financial services industry—brokerage, mutual fund investing, banking, insurance—is a lucrative, but frequently overlooked industry in discussions of advertising and marketing. The reason for this is the perception—the *image*—of the industry as suits, numbers crunchers and, in a word *boring*. The feeling is that banking hasn't changed much over the decades and that buying and selling stocks and bonds or leveraging one's investments tend to be subjects that are not for the masses or a great deal of visual interest. The occasional creative idea is watered down and hammered down by the legal department just to make sure there is nothing said or shown in an ad that might make anyone want to buy anything.

Financial services advertising used to require a somewhat sophisticated audience. Then a seasoned advertising pro pointed out that investors were consumers like everyone else and were subject to emotional responses. What followed were a generic series of Hallmark-like ads of old people in the park, young marrieds, graduation day, etc. The ads looked great, but they didn't distinguish Nuveen from Kemper from Merrill Lynch or Paine Webber. Although Merrill Lynch *did* have a bull in some of their ads to show it was "bullish" on America.

The Dreyfus lion walked around Wall Street, being a symbol of strength, speed and good instincts. Prudential said it was "rock solid" and to prove it, showed a rock. Metropolitan Life used the Charles Schulz "Peanuts" characters in a series of ads. It was sweet to see these beloved cartoon figures, even if no one quite understood why they were there.

Distinguished actor John Houseman appeared in a memorable ad for the investment firm Smith Barney ("We make money the old fashioned way—We *earn* it"), and, even years after his death, the firm is still remembered for it. How long that will be the case, no one can say. A mutual fund company created a series of TV ads in which it identified all the fear and confusion people feel when investing. Unfortunately, the company didn't offer the first clue to *solving* the problems.

Charles Schwab is a different kind of marketer. He offers no advice, just takes your order to the trading floor and enters it for a discounted fee. Schwab was, if not the first to do it, the first to nationally advertise discount brokerage service. The firm's other services are not significantly different from other full-service brokerage houses.

But Charles Schwab gave this advice to a new brokerage firm opening around 1980: put your picture in the ad and your name on the door. People like to know who's handling their money.

It may be a small point as image building goes, but consider the photograph in the ad and the brief appearance of the man in his TV commercials. He seems bright, pleasant-looking, well-spoken—even well-tailored when the coat is off and we see him standing confidently, arms folded, in that crisp white business shirt and necktie.

We don't know what Mr. Merrill looks like.

Or Lynch or Paine or Webber, and we know that the Dean Witter in those TV commercials is an actor. At least we *think* he is.

But we do think we know Charles Schwab. The tone of his ads is direct, down-to-earth, simple, no jokes or songs, but friendly. Next to his photograph in the magazine ads, Charles Schwab says, "To find out how Schwab can help you with all your investing needs, I invite you to stop by one of our more than 200 offices nationwide." You almost expect to find him in each one of the offices, waiting to shake your hand. You certainly get the feeling you can call him up and tell him what's on your mind if one of his people isn't on top of things. Several years ago, Charles Schwab sold his firm to the financial giant Bank of America. And a couple of years later, he bought it back from them. There was no public fireworks about it, but you got the sense that Mr. Schwab wanted to do things his own way. When he offers his slogan "Helping Investors Help Themselves" you believe he means it.

What will happen when he grows old, retires or dies remains to be seen. Maybe there's a Charles Jr. warming up in the bullpen. For now, Charles Schwab is America's most recognized broker because he put his picture in the ad. He thought you'd like to see who was handling your money.

Smart move.

SEARS
Most visible media: all

The question resonates with gloom: How can a store that is not just a *store,* but The Big Store—the one that called the radio station it owned WLS for "World's Largest Store"—seem to, in such a very short time, fall apart?

Sears Roebuck & Company's image was not the cause of its problems. But it was a lot more of a problem than Sears management ever seemed to understand or was willing to deal with. Once Sears was the approximation of a general store, with something for everyone, including a return policy that said it stood behind everything it sold. It seemed, too, that the stories were located in the heart of America's most populous urban centers as well as outlying areas.

Communities changed. People moved around—and away. Sears seemed hugely out of fashion, merchandise seemed "dated" and the return policy was discontinued for most of what Sears sold.

The Wall Street Journal called Donald R. Katz' book on Sears, *The Big Store,* "an epic tale of clashing egos and their impact on American business . . ."

The cover of the book's 1988 edition notes that "In 1972 Sears was the quintessential American success story . . . Two out of three Americans shopped there during any quarter of that year. Suddenly, Sears found itself in a downward spiral: profits plummeted, the stock prices collapsed, and civil war erupted within the corporation. By 1984, Sears was back on top, bigger than ever."

Alas, that was in 1988. Less than 10 years later, Sears was again fighting for its survival, believing that its management was moving in the proper direction in a business sense, but the Sears that had wrapped itself in advertising slogans like "Sears has everything" and "Where America shops" was clearly not the Sears of the future. Ironically, a Sears project called *The Store of the Future* proved to be one of its most significant failures. Sears was evolving in the minds of many to be a store very out of touch with what the public wanted.

The "department store" concept was said to be on its way out. Concept and specialty stores and boutiques were thought to be the future. The fact that department stores across the economic and geographic spectrum—Wal-Mart, Target and Nordstrom's, to name three—were growing and prospering, however, contradicted this theory.

As a retailer, Sears did better than anyone for years. Initially, the company built its reputation and its customer base in the catalog sales. The first Sears general merchandise catalog—The Big Book—in 1896 was truly a big book at 753 pages. It was also known over the years as The Dream Book and The Wish Book, helping to shape the American way of life and the American dream.

One indication of how badly Sears lost its way over the years is its decision, in 1992, to stop publishing The Big Book. Catalog sales that year totaled $3.3 billion. Yet, according to the *Chicago Tribune,* Sears posted after-tax losses of $135 million to $175 million each year between 1990 and 1992. Sears seemed unable to earn a profit in mail order at a time when this business it virtually invented was booming for its competitors.

As for the idea of Image Marketing, Sears seemed to largely ignore it, choosing instead to do what retailers have always done when business is bad: have a sale. Sort of.

The Sears "Everyday low prices" policy was a disaster, implying as it did that the store had been charging too much and now

was merely reacting to Wal-Mart and K-Mart's gains in market
share at Sears' expense. Sears had routinely dismissed such rivals
as mere irritants until it was too late.

Revisiting the idea of the Marketing Plan would likely have
helped Sears, if managers had left their egos at the door and looked
at the company honestly. A situation analysis would have revealed
that Sears' customer base had been changing, Sears' marketing
concepts were out-of-date and its stores were perceived as highly
out of fashion.

K-Mart ran "blue light specials," Marshall Field's continued
its fashion show luncheons, but added in-store appearances by
designers signing their products. And Sears, for its part, ran a lot
of ads and pretty much positioned itself in the same place it had
a half-century earlier, suggesting that it was quite enough for
Sears just to be Sears. Forget the specialty stores. Sears had
something for everybody, provided that everybody was about forty
years old, had been so for a long time and planned to stay that
way, displaying no interest in style or fashion.

One of the very few positive chapters in the Sears story came
with its recognition of the value and power it held in its charge-
cardholder base, estimated at some 24 million names and accounts. By offering this group a more all-purpose credit card, the
Discover Card, Sears offered its customers the service of its bank
. . . while they shopped elsewhere.

In the 1990s, Sears had launched, with reasonable success,
a new line of "specialty catalogs" with titles like *Unique Expressions, Smart Choice, Right Touch* . . . in pursuit of the market that
had deserted it for *Lands' End, Victoria's Secret* and other emerging shop-at-home leaders.

Sears' image had become about equal to that of a nearby
mailbox—useful, convenient, but totally unexciting. This is not a
good definition of a successful retailer.

Sears had stopped listening to the voice of the market. Its
customers felt this and responded accordingly. If it is to make yet
another comeback, it will be because it fashions an image of a
brighter, stylish, service-oriented entity, working around what it
has to offer today, not what it was a century ago. Companies with
fewer resources and bigger problems than Sears have experienced

successful turnarounds . . . with the public cheering them on. Sears must effectively address the public's perception of it in order for the cheering to start. But that can't be done by insisting on doing things that haven't worked. Sears obviously has done the research and sees what its competitors are doing, but reacting to sale prices, decor or ad spending is neither enough or a well-chosen course. In addition to these moves, Sears must attempt to change people's perceptions. The ad line "There's more for your life at Sears" needs to be reflected, not just stated.

By the fall of 1995, with a new management team in place that believed respect for Sears' historic corporate culture was not the same as deference to it, major changes were underway. Sears had some 800 large department stores in malls and 1,200 off-mall stores. The focus was very customer-specific in various communities, giving the community what it wanted. The numbers and faces of the outlet stores tell the story of the image the new management team sought to convey: 125 Homelife stores; 86 Sears Hardware outlets; 655 Western Auto Stores; and more than 300 rural stores operated by local independent dealers.

Presenting an image of "where America shops" must first take into account, store by store, what America *wants*. After a long period of silence, Sears once again seemed to be listening.

STARBUCKS COFFEE
Most visible medium: point-of-sale

The price of coffee seems to be going up almost continuously. It's been a long time since anyone has asked for "a dime for a cup of coffee."

Anyway, your doctor keeps saying it's bad for you and you should cut back to a cup a day or quit drinking it altogether.

With such a scenario as this to start with, it would not seem like a great time to go into the coffee business, much less to launch a chain of specialty coffee shops and cafes.

An English teacher, a history teacher, and a writer founded Starbucks in 1971, when they were taken with the mood of the

Berkeley, California coffee house scene. The name, they claim, was to honor the coffee-loving first-mate in Herman Melville's *Moby Dick*. Enthusiastic, but admittedly, unfocused, the owners recruited a brilliant young marketing man named Howard Schultz, who joined them in 1982. Mr. Schultz introduced the concept of integrated marketing to Starbucks and five years later, with the help of investors, bought Starbucks from its founders for $4 million. Despite slow starts and three straight years of losses, Starbucks' first eleven stores grew to nearly 500 in less than a dozen years. When the company went public in 1991, it quickly became, in the words of *Advertising Age,* "The Darling of Wall Street." Starbucks' goal of 6,000 outlets by the turn of the century impressed analysts as realistic.

A San Francisco investment banker noted, "They don't market. They've established a major presence all through word-of-mouth. They are not a traditional consumer products company."

They may be nontraditional, but it's not correct to say Starbucks doesn't market itself. Rather, like legendary athletes and entertainers, they appear to market so effortlessly, you don't see it happening while you're watching it.

Starbucks serves more than 13 million customers a week. While the media budget may be small in relation to the company's image, Mr. Schultz seems ready to meet the challenges ahead. Refusing to use artificially flavored beans, he notes that customers first "must recognize you do stand for something."

From the first outdoor boards, brochures and point-of-sales displays that used an architectural drawing of how Starbucks specialty coffee was prepared, the company's marketing grew into catalogs, coupons and some direct mail. Starbucks Specialty Sales & Marketing Group began cultivating restaurant and connoisseur businesses with small ads in *The New Yorker.* The distinctive paper cups with oversized lids have become almost a status symbol for Starbucks carry-out customers. Embossed mugs and cups of odd shapes and sizes—all, however, showing the Starbucks logo—sell briskly, as do coffeemakers and an ever-expanding line of Starbucks foods, beans, books and whatever can be developed to catch the fancy of customers once they are inside the door.

"The marketing of Starbucks is not only what people see on the outside," Mr. Schultz notes. "The cost of internal marketing is quite high, but it is the key to our success."

The New York Times reported that "The Specialty Coffee Association of America predicts that the number of specialty coffee cafes in the country (0 in 1969) will reach 10,000 by 1999."

Starbucks chose its locations carefully, concentrating on upscale locations, whether they be in malls, shopping districts or hotels. In a tough economy, customers lined up to pay up to $4 for a carry-out paper cup of strong coffee or cappucino. Like the BMW and the Rolex watch, the taste for the finer things was there to be tapped and Starbucks did it.

VICTORIA'S SECRET
Most visible media: direct mail, point-of-sale

Sex sells, the expression goes, and countless marketing entities have used sex or attempts at sex appeal to get attention and generate product interest. For a "respectable" mainstream enterprise, attempting to use sex in marketing can be a very risky proposition.

The expression "sex sells" is often applied to advertising that, while erotic, is not necessarily regarded as tasteful or dignified. Victoria's Secret is the exception. With an expanding chain of retail stores and an exploding catalog business, the company has masterfully navigated a course between the elegant, pricey and somewhat elitist tone of fashion boutiques, and the flamboyant intimacy of, say, Frederick's of Hollywood. Victoria's Secret nightwear, clothing and accessories emphasize elegance and good taste, and yet the company clearly pushes the limits of good taste in catalog photographs that invite a "can-you-see-yourself-in-this-picture?" romantic fantasy.

As lingerie goes, it is perhaps the most intimate line of its era. It is also an example of the theory that "less is more." The company has a very much understated profile. With a mainstay product line that is primarily intimate apparel—and a trademark promotional vehicle of stunning catalog photos—the risk exists of crossing the line to tasteless exploitation.

Victoria's Secret succeeded in its category for many of the same reasons Playboy succeeded in its original category. Victoria's "secret" was in the simple recognition that many women secretly wanted to dress for romantic moments in lingerie that was surely somewhat erotic, but more sensuous. The choices offered by the finer stores were often very limited and very costly. The alternative seemed to be only the other extreme: trashy to the point of embarrassment, both to purchase and display. There seemed to be virtually nothing readily available in between.

The Sears Roebuck catalog is credited with being the beginning of mass mail order retailing. It used to be called "The Dream Book" and "The Wish Book," as people would look at the catalog and fantasize about owning the items that filled its pages. Sears halted production of its catalog, saying that in the modern era, it was no longer as profitable or as cost-effective as it needed to be. Curiously, this announcement coincided with a virtual boom in home shopping and mail order buying. The Victoria's Secret catalog inherited the mantle of "The Dream Book."

Without question, millions of women (and probably many men) considered the photographs of the beautiful models exemplary of what advertising was all about—the stuff of fantasies. A typical 100-page color catalog would include several pages of sweaters, slacks and fragrance products (and the stores would even feature tapes and CDs of romantic music), but it was the items of intimate apparel that were the essence of the catalog. And of the store's point-of-sale displays. And, indeed, the company.

The word "sexy" doesn't appear once anywhere. It doesn't have to. Instead are descriptions of items *luxurious, silky, romantic, dramatic, sensual* and *classic.*

The stores' decor is tasteful, English-influenced and reserved enough for the teenage male shopper to feel unself-conscious while gift shopping. Almost. For the more discreet shoppers, the catalog does it.

Rather than being the product of mass media, the Victoria's Secret image has been largely catalog-driven and direct mail

E X H I B I T   9 . 2

Victoria's Secret

Can you see yourself in this picture? Victoria's Secret offers a catalog that becomes a "wish book" with beautiful women in beautiful, mostly intimate apparel. Fantasies tastefully reflected in the privacy of your home—and the clothes are affordable.

enhanced. Its catalog pass-along and word-of-mouth referrals are worthy of a multi-level marketing sales effort. The primary medium is the mailbox; the image and message is affordable elegance and good taste . . . unselfconsciously sexy. It appears to be the company's direct avoidance of a loud media campaign that works in its favor, similar to the operating style of The Body Shop and certainly successful.

A Crash Course in Image Marketing

The Body Shop, Ben & Jerry's and Starbucks are three very young, successful venture companies. None of them is a major advertiser in the traditional media advertising sense: all three use some direct mail, but rely largely on heavy point-of-sale, public relations and word-of-mouth promotion. Indeed, a large part of each company's PR and positioning statement makes a high-profile point of the fact that they advertise so little or don't advertise at all. Note that each of these companies positions itself as the purveyor of premium products. While they would obviously love to have everyone's business, they insist on making a dramatic point that they are not for everybody, but only for the most discriminating of customers . . .

. . . Who have five dollars to spend.

And customers appear inclined to spend their last five dollars to show the rest of the public that they are indeed of discriminating tastes.

In his humor book *Read My Clips,* Lewis Grossberger presents this observation as a question on the discriminating, elitist segment of American society: Does hip mean only up-to-the-minute trendiness? Or does it require an attitude involving some degree of opposition to the prevailing ethos? Isn't *hipness* largely about being an outsider?"

Sophisticated has a nice sound to it, but Image Marketers should know that hipness and *trendiness* carry a suggestion that you're the brand of choice for now, but, perhaps, you're not here for the long haul.

Know, too, in creating an image that the culture does now—and perhaps did always—have a seeming affinity for the word *change.* Every politician offers it, the situation seems to worsen after each election, yet the public still responds and pledges support to anyone who stands for change the next time around as well. Change tends to be seen as inevitable, healthy, positive, lamented and feared.

The value-weighting system seems subject to periodic reconsideration as well. Once to put the word unlimited after a business name meant to suggest there was no limitation on one's capability to deliver. Modern times prefer the word limited at the end of an enterprise to provide a certain cache, sense of exclusivity or uniqueness. A commodity's being "unlimited" no longer seems necessarily to be a point in its favor.

Consider that in Image Marketing no one approach is best for everyone. The Body Shop and Starbucks may be growing without traditional advertising, but that doesn't mean traditional advertising isn't effective to create or enhance an image. It is no mere coincidence that America's largest companies are the country's biggest advertisers—and it's not just because they have the money to be. It is a reflection of the fact that virtually any advertising will help you become better known and move product. Good advertising well-created, running enough times in the right media will succeed dramatically in most cases.

The "most cases" qualifier is there because history has shown, regardless of how strong and well-regarded a name might be, you still can't sell a product nobody wants. Pepsi, for example, is a name with both cache and clout in the marketplace—a great image, plenty of financing and a strong base. That, however, wasn't enough to make successes of Crystal Pepsi, Pepsi A.M., Pepsi X.L., and a couple of the company's other products that seemed like a good idea to the marketing department, but the public just wasn't interested.

While direct mail still seems to be the vehicle of choice for fundraising, increasingly cause marketing efforts are being augmented by a very traditional full-page ad placed in the *New York Times* and other large local papers, where fundraisers include coupons and 800-numbers to encourage potential contributors to respond. While the ad itself raises awareness, increases visibility and presents a desired image in a controlled space, which in turn leads to money coming in. The National Committee to Prevent Child Abuse, Anti-Defamation League, Committee Against Political Corruption and the Sea Turtle Restoration Project are only a few of the groups that have employed this technique. While costly, it does afford the advantage of presenting a point of view, claim and testimonials without affording critics or opposing views a forum.

Public awareness occurs for a variety of reasons, from a full-page ad in a newspaper to a one-shot appearance on a TV talk show to being involved in a home videotape that finds its way on to the news. How that awareness is managed to create, define and maintain an image for marketing purposes, whether a product, service, company, profession, industry or association, is deliberate and serious. You may get your TV shot—your fifteen minutes of fame—but without the proper preparation and the maximization of the fifteen minutes, you may not get a chance at another fifteen minutes.

Here is a basic outline to help create a framework to create, present and maintain a public image of who you are and what you represent:

1. **Do current attitude and awareness research.**

   A most basic element of success is knowledge. Know what all of your constituent groups (customers, clients, dealers, employees, regulators, shareholders) think of you, your competition and your industry or profession. Dated research that does not reflect the current situation accurately is useless or, at the very least, misleading.

2. Question research.

Researchers understand that people frequently answer
questions the way they think they should or give the
answers the researcher's looking for. This extends to
employees and family. Ford's Edsel, Pepsi A.M. and
microwave meals all presumably came out of extensive
market research that proved at least somewhat
unreliable. Test and double-check. The stakes are too
high not to.

3. Be "out there."

Creating and sustaining an image does not allow for
waiting for someone to come to you. You must take the
initiative to make your presence known. By coming
forward you increase your prospects of controlling the
agenda or the content vs. reacting to questions or
comments someone else has determined or defined.

4. Be sincere.

Many companies and individuals are taking positions
that give the appearance of political and social
correctness. That these positions seem contrived,
calculated and insincere carries the potential the effort
may backfire and cause major image damage. Being
"green"—environmentally friendly—is fine if it is a
sincere commitment. Tobacco companies running ads
that try to discourage kids from smoking and breweries
running anti-drinking ads appear designed to head-off
restrictive legislation under the guise of public concern.
Nobody's fooled.

5. Clearly define the image you aspire to have.

It was fine for the old TV commercial to speculate
whether Certs was a candy or a breath mint, but to
market your image effectively, you must be clear in
your presentation, so that the media or, worse, your
competitors don't define who you are and where you fit.

6. Stress benefits and your uniqueness.

People want to know what's in it for them. Why should they support you, patronize you, refer others to you or care about you at all? Skip the claims about how you are the biggest, best, oldest, most listened-to, etc. Such showboating, full-of-yourself claims might make *you* feel more important, but remember the target. People to whom you are marketing should hear about benefits, guarantees and specific proof of quality—not just a general claim of quality.

7. Define your audience.

Know who you are marketing to. The time has passed when the same toothpaste, shampoo, beverage or chewing gum is likely to be the choice of everyone. Targeting your message to your audience saves in virtually every respect. If your market is older, younger, male, female, sophisticated, conservative, rural or urban—know it and let your marketing reflect it.

8. Create and use a marketing plan.

Even the most seasoned travellers use a map. Your marketing plan should include these essential elements: *situation analysis, objectives, strategy and tactics, timeline and budget.* You can't "stay on track" if you don't know what your track looks like or where it is supposed to go. Similarly, know and understand what marketing and its components (advertising, public relations, etc.) can and cannot do. Be realistic.

9. Create and maintain a steady flow of information.

To create or change perceptions, you can't just wait for something that favors you to happen. Generate ads, press releases, story ideas, surveys, position papers. Offer opinions and comment on research and opinions of others, particularly competitors. That doesn't mean

criticize competitors, it means respond and expand upon
their information.

10. Be specific in your information.

Politicians and marketers can get some attention by
being ever-present with a statement or opinion about
what's wrong. So what? To succeed and separate
yourself, your product or company from the rest, you
must clearly be specific about why people should
patronize or support you. Offer a better—or at least an
original idea. Just being there, claiming to be generally
better, or criticizing will get a bit of attention, but not
much more.

11. Be respectful of other people's time.

When making contact with members of the media, do
not suggest your time is more valuable than theirs.

12. Don't overpromise or overstate your cause.

In building an image, a certain amount of hype is
expected, too much is deadly (note the Apple computer
story).

13. Don't wear out your welcome.

Make your case directly, honestly; follow-up, but don't
push or oversell. Your goal is to win goodwill, not to be
persistent to the point of annoyance.

14. Resist the temptation to reduce your marketing budget when business is either very good or very bad—these are the times you need it most.

15. Be patient.

Images—perceptions—are rarely made or changed
overnight. Have faith in your plan and pursue it.

16. Do well by doing good.

Embrace a cause that will show you are a good and
caring part of your local and corporate community.

17. Make your support of a cause fit your own image and business.

Not only must your support for a good cause—whether AIDS research or Little League—be legitimate and sincere, but it should fit what you do. Ben & Jerry's puts a portion of profits into the small farms and underdeveloped regions where it buys products; The Body Shop fights against animal testing in research for products its industry produces. Pharmaceutical companies offer research grants. These fit and help promote an image of concern about and within an industry and community. When Sears' marketing chief told a reporter that Sears' sponsorship of a rock star's concert that will help raise money for homeless people "will reinforce the idea that Sears is the most compelling place to shop" it destroyed a major image benefit to Sears by stressing it was involved primarily for publicity.

18. The first rule of effective public relations is to be good.

Be realistic about what your Image Marketing program can achieve. PR people can usually find something good to say about almost anyone or anything. But you can't look good unless you are good. Hiring a PR person to cover your misdeeds is usually futile, costly and doomed to embarrassment.

19. Be honest.

The public respects people who back up their claims, distrusts people who don't and tends to forgive and allow another chance to those who admit mistakes and take responsibility.

20. Celebrity spokespeople can both help and hurt.

A celebrity endorsement can help get more attention faster. It can also help win, by association, the goodwill of the celebrity's fans. But, because it is common knowledge that celebrities often are paid large endorsement fees, the celebrity's credibility may be at issue. The sponsor's image may also be helped or hurt by the public and private life of the celebrity—positively from awards or success, negatively from a scandal or crisis in the celebrity's life. Make the celebrity an appropriate match to the entity he or she is going to be asked to endorse; make the fee fit the budget; recognize you are together in the public's mind for better or worse.

21. Humor in marketing can be risky.

As with a celebrity, humorous touches in ads, PR programs and promotions can help get attention faster, but run a risk of offending some people, alienating others, perhaps even just striking others as not funny. Remember the point is to create a positive image. The approach should be consistent with your risk tolerance level.

22. Image Marketing overlaps practice and budget areas.

Your image should be reflected in all elements of your marketing—signage, letterhead, ads, catalogs, trucks, vans, shipping materials, grants or contributions and memberships.

23. Think of your image in media choices.

Whether buying media, accepting a speaking invitation or an award or being interviewed or profiled, where you appear is as important as *that* you appear—perhaps more so. Every exposure should be in a place that helps to reflect the image you are seeking to present.

24. Merchandise your presence.

Ads, newsletters, surveys, appointments, speeches, articles, books, interviews—even your percentage of shelf-space—are all potential subjects for merchandising and promotion. Extend each to its maximum level of exploitation.

25. Create a reservoir of goodwill.

In advancing your image or in times of crisis, it's good to have friends. Being an active and involved part of your community both enhances your image and builds a treasury of good works that you may want to refer to at a later date.

26. Avoid the negative option.

In ads, speeches, interviews, literature and other PR materials, avoid insults, attacks, and criticism of your competitors or opponents. Among the reasons for this are that the public and most professions prefer dignity over nastiness and tend to favor those who "take the high road." Stress instead the value and benefits of what you have to offer. Let your efforts be customer-driven, rather than prompted by the irresistible urge to bash the competition. Such comments get short term attention and breed long-term ill will. Remember that if the best thing you can say about what you have to offer is something negative about your competition, you have a serious problem with what you have to offer.

27. Avoid comparisons.

It used to be "Brand X," "other leading brands," or "my worthy opponent." Alas, in a time of bad manners and attack ads, competitors are cited by name and often shown as well. Forget it. Skip the comparisons for all the reasons noted in the preceding point and one more: why publicize a competitor *at all* when you've paid for or otherwise control the space? Make better use of it by working *your* messages.

28. Think perceptions—images.

Can recognition or success be bought? Probably not. But the perception can. Consider: *The Best Dressed List, The Top Ten, The Man of the Year, The Woman of the Year, The Beautiful People, The Most Eligible, Who's hot/who's new.* These are all examples of publicists at

work to create the perception that recognition and
success exist.

29. Images are emotional. Think "emotions."
Pretty much all the forms of overt marketing—
advertising, public relations, promotions—will help
insure *that* people think of you. Image Marketing will
influence *how* people think of you and what they do
about it. Offer the list of unique features and benefits of
what you are presenting and representing. Be sincere.
But know that what triggers emotional responses—a
smile, a warm or sentimental feeling, excitement,
shock, pride, amazement, recognition, satisfaction—are
moments people remember. Long after a specific great
ad campaign has stopped, the package discarded and
the brochure yellowed with age, perceptions and images
remain. Protect them and they can prove to be very
good to you.

BIBLIOGRAPHY
AND REFERENCE

Advertising Age November 7, 1994 "Our Changing Lifestyles"; June 27, 1994 "Sponsors can't hide," an editorial; June 27, 1994 "O.J. Case casts pall on endorsers"; November 14, 1994 "What to do with a fallen star"; Spring, 1995 "50 Years of TV Advertising"; November 14, 1994 "What's wrong with negative ads?" by Rance Crain; October 10, 1994 "Body Shop marches to its own drummer" by Charles Siler; "Roddick skewers critics"; February 6, 1995 "Yo! Ben & Jerry's finds a CEO with taste for verse" by Pat Sloan; September 26, 1994 "Social marketing misses the mark" by Rance Crain; February 6, 1995 "Benetton, German retailers squabble" by Dagmar Mussey; August 1, 1994 "Chastened Newton turns 1 with hope intact" by Bradley Johnson; November 21, 1994 "New Magic Needed for Disney Kingdom" by Christy Fisher; August 15, 1994 "Newton Marketing Lessons" an editorial; March 7, 1994 "Starbucks word-of-mouth wonder" by Alice Z. Cuneo.

Barabba, Vincent P. and Gerald Zaltman, 1991, *Hearing the Voice of the Market*. Boston: Harvard Business School Press.

Brady, James. 1974. *Superchic*. New York: Little, Brown & Company.

Business Week March 2, 1994 "Behind the scandal at Spectrum" by
     Michael Schroder; March 21, 1994 "Are good causes good
     marketing?"

Chicago Tribune June 25, 1995 "Logic and Mr. Limbaugh" by
     Clarence Peterson; March 23, 1995 "A cheerleader for lawyers"
     by Laura Duncan; May 30, 1995 "A new tack: law firm gives
     written service guarantees" by James Hanna, John O'Brien and
     Bill Crawford; July 9, 1995 "Sears new little books tell big
     success story?" by Genevieve Buck.

Colors March, 1995. "What the hell is this magazine?" published by
     Benetton.

Dilenschneider, Robert L. 1990. *Power and Influence.* New York:
     Prentice Hall Press.

Freberg, Stan. 1988. *It Only Hurts When I Laugh.* New York: Times
     Books.

Gershman, Michael. 1990. *Getting It Right the Second Time.* San
     Francisco: Addison-Wesley Publishing.

Gregory, James R. 1993. *Seven Steps to Improving Your Corporate
     Image.* Stamford, CT: Gregory & Clyburne, Inc.

Gregory, James R. with Jack G. Wiechmann. 1991. *Marketing
     Corporate Image.* Chicago: NTC Business Books.

Grossberger, Lewis. 1991. *Read My Clips.* New York: Random House.

Hughes, Robert. 1991. *Culture of Complaint.* New York: Warner
     Books.

Information Week October 17, 1994 "Ours to Lose" by Katherine Bull.

Katz, Donald R. 1987. *The Big Store.* New York: Penguin Books.

Lager, Fred. 1994. *Ben & Jerry's: The Inside Scoop.* New York: Crown
     Publishers.

Lesley, Philip. 1991. *Lesley's Handbook of Public Relations and
     Communications.* Chicago: Probus Publishing.

Lytle, John F. 1993. *What Do Customers Really Want?* Chicago:
     Probus Publishing.

Maltese, John Anthony. 1992. *Spin Control.* Chapel Hill: University of
     North Carolina Press.

Marconi, Joe. 1991. *Getting the Best from Your Ad Agency.* Chicago:
     Probus Publishing.

McGinnis, Joe. 1969. *The Selling of the President 1968.* New York: Trident Press.

Meyers, William. 1984. *The Image Makers: Power and Persuasion on Madison Avenue.* New York: Times Books.

Naisbitt, John and Patricia Aburdene. 1990. *Mega-Trends 2000.* New York: William Morrow and Company.

New York Times December 28, 1994 "The Year Beef Came Back" by Suzanne Hamlin; April 18, 1995 "Religion goes to the market to expand congregations" by Gustav Nieburk; June 8, 1995 "Why is this surgeon suing?" by Sabra Chartand; May 26, 1995 "Fistfuls of coupons" by Marry Meier; June 20, 1995 "Thoughts Uplifting and Folksy" by Stephen Holden; April 9, 1995 "Clouds over Disneyland" by Bernard Weinraub; April 23, 1995 "Six Facts" on coffee.

Ogilvy, David. 1983. *Ogilvy on Advertising.* New York: Crown Books.

O'Toole, John. 1980. *The Trouble with Advertising.* New York: Chelsea House Publishing.

Ries, Al and Jack Trout. 1993. *The 22 Immutable Laws of Marketing.* New York: Harper Business.

Rogers, Henry. 1980. *Walking the Tightrope.* New York: William Morrow and Company.

Schulberg, Bob. *Radio Advertising,* 2nd ed., rev. Peter Schulberg. Chicago: NTC Business Books, 1996.

Sculley, John. 1987. *Odyssey: Pepsi to Apple . . . The Journey of a Marketing Impresario.* New York: Harper & Row Publishers.

CREDITS

Exhibit 1:1. *Rolling Stone* "Perception. Reality." © by Straight Arrow Publishers, Inc. 1987. All Rights Reserved. Reprinted by Permission.

Exhibit 2:1. SunGard "You've Come to the Right Place." Courtesy of SunGard Trust and Shareholder Systems. Jareo Jareo Marketing Communications.

Exhibit 2:2. The Options Industry Council "the Options Tool." Courtesy of The Options Industry Council.

Exhibit 2:3. Deloitte & Touche "Everything you want to know about your competitors in one fell swoop." Deloitte Touche Tohmatsu International. Courtesy of Deloitte Touche LLP.

Exhibit 3:1. Swiss Army Watch "Built like our Swiss Army Knife." © 1994 Swiss Army Brands Ltd., a subsidiary of The Forschner Group, Inc. Used by permission.

Exhibit 3:2. *The Harvard Business Review*. "There is no denying the Review's importance." Courtesy of The Harvard Business Review. Harvard Business School Publishing.

Exhibit 4:1. Elizabeth Taylor White Diamonds "The fragrance dreams are made of." © 1995 Parfums International Ltd. Elizabeth Arden. Photograph: Bruce Weber.

Exhibit 4:3. Swatch "There would be no world records, no thrill of victory, no gold medals. Time. Without it there would be no Olympic Games." Swatch Watches.

Exhibit 7:2. Riverside Square "Riverside style at work." Courtesy of Keroff & Rosenberg Advertising.

Exhibit 7:3. Riverside Square "Riverside Square Presents Decorating with Antiques." Courtesy of Keroff & Rosenberg Advertising.

Exhibit 7:4. The Shops at the Mart "Warhol." Courtesy of Keroff & Rosenberg Advertising.

Exhibit 7:5. Aurora Health Care "It's all about people." © 1994 Aurora Health Care. Courtesy of Bender Browning Dolby & Sanderson Advertising.

Exhibit 9:1. Disney. Photo: Karin Gottschalk.

Exhibit 9:2. Victoria's Secret. Photo: Karin Gottschalk.

ABOUT THE AUTHOR

JOE MARCONI is a marketing communications consultant with more than two decades of award-winning advertising, public relations and marketing programs and campaigns to his credit. He has been both a corporate communications executive and principal of a major national agency.

A frequent lecturer and marketing communications seminar leader throughout the United States and Canada, Mr. Marconi's writing has appeared in numerous publications, including the *International Herald Tribune,* the *Chicago Tribune* and *Research Magazine.* He is the author of the international best-selling business books *Getting the Best from Your Ad Agency* (1991), *Crisis Marketing: When Bad Things Happen to Good Companies* (1992) and *Beyond Branding* (1993), as well as a contributor to a number of collections. He lives in Western Springs, Illinois, near Chicago.

INDEX

American Marketing Association

The American Marketing Association, the world's largest and most comprehensive professional association of marketers, has over 40,000 members worldwide and over 500 chapters throughout North America. It sponsors 25 major conferences per year, covering topics ranging from the latest trends in customer satisfaction measurement to business-to-business and services marketing, to attitude research and sales promotion. The AMA publishes 9 major marketing publications, including *Marketing Management*, a quarterly magazine aimed at marketing managers, and dozens of books addressing special issues, such as relationship marketing, marketing research, and entrepreneurial marketing for small and home-based businesses. Let the AMA be your strategy for success.

For further information on the American Marketing Association, call TOLL FREE at 1-800-AMA-1150.

Or write to
American Marketing Association
250 S. Wacker Drive, Suite 200
Chicago, Illinois 60606
(312) 648-0536
(312) 993-7542 FAX